the best man's
speech & duties

the best man's

speech & duties

hamlyn

confetti.co.uk

First published in Great Britain in 2007 by
Hamlyn, a division of Octopus Publishing Group Ltd
2–4 Heron Quays, London E14 4JP

ISBN-13: 978-0-600-61646-7
ISBN-10: 0-600-61646-0

A CIP catalogue record for this book is available from
the British Library

Printed and bound in China

10 9 8 7 6 5 4 3 2

contents

Introduction

So, you've been asked to be a best man – congratulations! You will no doubt be feeling elated, honoured and maybe even a little emotional at being chosen for this pivotal role. However, as these feelings begin to fade, they may well be replaced by a sense of panic and dread at just what you've taken on. If that's the case, don't worry; it's perfectly normal and this book is here to help.

Being a best man is an event that is unlikely to occur more than once or maybe twice in your life so naturally you want to do a good job. You also want to justify the couple's decision to pick you and, above all, do your best to ensure their day runs as smoothly as possible. As best man, you have a number of key responsibilities in the lead-up to the wedding and on the day itself. It's your job to deal with all those last-minute problems and hitches so that the bride and groom are able to relax and enjoy themselves. As well as these practical duties, you will also be on hand to offer support and reassurance to the groom, acting as a calming influence when things get hectic, and they will!

This practical book covers everything you need to know about your duties as best man, from co-ordinating the ushers to arranging a great stag night and it will also be your indispensable guide in the run-up to the big day. Each chapter takes you through a key stage of your role in the wedding, offering plenty of helpful tips and advice along the way. The first chapter deals with the best man's responsibilities in the months before the wedding – yes there are plenty, such as getting the family together for a wedding meeting and helping to choose the ushers. In the second chapter you'll find all the ideas and inspiration you need to organize the perfect stag night, which is your biggest pre-wedding job. The third chapter covers all your duties on the day itself, from picking up buttonholes to arranging transport to the reception. In chapters four to seven you'll be guided through the all-important (and often dreaded) speech and toast. There are tips on preparation, nerves and delivery techniques, as well as jokes, one-liners and sample speeches. By the time it's your turn to take the floor, you'll be ready to wow them!

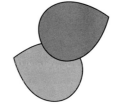

For more ideas and resources, why not visit our website (www.confetti.co.uk). There you will find expert advice on your duties as best man and inspiring ideas for your speech.

Duties before the wedding day

As you'll soon discover, the best man's job starts well before the stag night. Your tasks are many and varied but essentially, during the run-up to the wedding, the groom will rely on you for support and help with organization. As best man, you need to be a troubleshooter and an entertainer, act as a chapter on on the stag night and, above all, be a loyal friend to the groom.

Overseeing the proceedings

The best man is one of the key figures in the wedding ritual. Not only do you play an important role in the weeks leading up to the event (particularly on the groom's side), but you also oversee the whole day itself in the capacity of 'Master of Ceremonies'.

Reasons for accepting/declining

Acceptable reasons for refusing the role
- A prior engagement on the day
- A previous liaison with the bride
- Illness or disability
- You don't know the groom that well and are not sure why you've been asked (but don't give this as a reason!)

If in doubt, refuse in time for someone else to be asked and before money has been spent.

Unacceptable reasons for refusing the role
- You don't have any respect for the bride
- You just don't want to have to organize the stag night
- You get a better offer for that day later on
- You can't afford it

Once you've accepted, it's important that the groom feels he can rely on you for ongoing support, especially on the day.

Family

Call a family huddle

Arranging a 'family huddle' is a good idea. Get together with the groom, bride and her parents to find out how you can help prepare for the wedding. If you don't already know each other, it's also a chance to meet before the big day. The earlier the chat, the better, so that everyone is given the chance to have their say, and jobs and duties can be allocated.

Create a pleasant environment for the conversation – a meal out, perhaps – and explain beforehand the point of the meeting, so that everyone has the opportunity to gather their thoughts. If possible, visit the bride and groom's chosen ceremony and reception venues. By familiarizing yourself with the layouts you'll feel much more prepared on the day. To ensure the smooth running of play on the day, it might be wise to note things like timings between venues, locations of entrances and exits, car-parking facilities and access, particularly if there will be disabled guests.

Dress rehearsal
You'll definitely need to turn up to any wedding run-through that's been planned. This will give you a chance to familiarize yourself with the layout of the venue and get a better grasp of your role in the proceedings. Just knowing exactly where to stand and what to do on the big day will help soothe your nerves. The rehearsal may also be a good chance for you to make sure that the fees are paid in advance to all those involved in the ceremony including the registrar, organist, bell-ringers, singers and musicians.

Know your team

Organizing the ushers

Traditionally, the groom and best man get together to choose the ushers, although the groom might want to do this by himself. As best man, you need to make sure the ushers are aware of their responsibilities, that they recognize the key family members and are generally charming and helpful on the day. They should also be aware – thanks to you – of any special seating requirements, such as guests in wheelchairs, who may need extra space and perhaps help getting to their places. Ushers should also make sure that the seats at the front of the ceremony venue reserved for close family members are not taken by other guests.

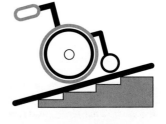

What does an usher do?

It's a good idea to brief ushers of what to expect:

- Make sure they are available for any fittings for their suit (if necessary) and for the stag night.
- They may be required to attend the wedding rehearsal. This is an opportunity for them not only to meet the members of the wedding party, but also to get an understanding of what's going to happen at the actual ceremony.

- Although their duties on the day may be relatively light, ushers should be available to help the best man out when and where they can. This could mean assisting any guests in wheelchairs to their place at the venue, slipping away in advance to light the lanterns for a winter wedding procession or even helping to hand round food or drinks.

- An ideal usher will be a Jeeves-like presence at the wedding, calmly and politely ironing out any last-minute creases and adding greatly to the smooth running of the day. They also usually act as escorts to the bridesmaids during the course of the day!

What they should wear

As befits their 'staff status', ushers will want to dress in the style of the groom and best man. So, if the groom is in morning dress, the ushers will be, too, although perhaps they'll have a flower buttonhole of a different colour from the groom and best man.

The wedding morning

It's a good idea for you and the ushers to meet at the wedding venue some time before the ceremony and well before the arrival of any early guests. Here, they can collect buttonholes and the service sheets, synchronize watches and discuss any other relevant issues. Ask ushers to bring an umbrella, too, just in case they need to escort guests to and from their transport in the rain.

During the ceremony

Make sure ushers recognize the 'key players' at the wedding, especially the parents.

Having ushers from the bride's side and also from the groom's will greatly help here, as well as contributing in a practical way to the symbolic union of two families, which a wedding represents.

Seating the guests

Give the ushers a seating plan for the front rows and brief them about any family friction that may need to be negotiated. If there's a chief usher, he will delegate the other tasks, such as giving out the service sheets. Be aware of any elderly or disabled guests who could use some help. At least one usher should stand at the back during the service, to welcome latecomers and discreetly guide them to a spare seat. You may also want to ask ushers to seat parents with small babies near doors, so they can make a quick exit if they need to!

Bride's to the left... At least one of the ushers will stand at the foot of the aisle to ask guests on which side they are to sit. Don't forget: groom's friends and family on the right, bride's on the left.

Mid-field usher Another usher should position himself halfway down the aisle to guide people to their seats. This is easier said than done, however, since they will be trying to get guests with babies into the aisle seats and directing tall people to places where they won't be obscuring other people's views!

Escorting the bride's mother The chief usher will be posted at the church door to escort the bride's mother to her seat on arrival at the church. She should be the last to take her seat before the entrance of the bridal party.

After the ceremony

Outside the wedding venue, ushers can help to find specific guests for the photographer's pictures, or – more likely – to help organize transport for the guests from the wedding venue to the reception.

At the reception

Once at the reception venue, ushers can start to relax a little and enjoy the party, although there may still be some small jobs they can perform – perhaps to help with the efficient flow of food and drink. When the guests arrive at the reception, the ushers should direct them to the room where the bride and groom would like them to assemble. If traditional dancing takes place, it is usually the ushers who dance with the bridesmaids for the second dance.

Arranging the transport

You may have to arrange the transport for the wedding day. Make sure you discuss the arrangements fully with the bride and her parents. Remember not all brides opt for the conventional way of travelling to the ceremony by car. If that's the case, you may be able to help organize whatever mode of transport she has chosen. However, if she is going by car, discuss with the bride's parents how many cars will be needed and ask if they'd like you to get quotes and make the booking. An average order would be two cars from the bride's home to the ceremony venue and three from there to the reception – the third car being for the newlyweds.

Crucially, it's your job to get the groom to the venue on time and in one piece and it would be wise to talk him out of any unusual ways of arriving at the venue! You may prefer to rely on your own transport and make sure you have the number of a local taxi firm in case you or any guests run into any problems. Also, carry maps to the venues and if you don't have a mobile phone, borrow one. Just make sure it's switched off during the ceremony.

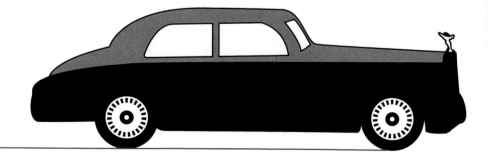

Travelling in style

Although it's not usual, the bride may even consult you for ideas about how to make her all-important journey to the wedding. Although a vintage Rolls or Daimler is the traditional and certainly the most glamorous way to arrive at a wedding, there are some weird and wonderful alternatives you could suggest!

- Classy motor – A stretch limousine adds a dash of Hollywood glamour to the proceedings. Alternatively, consider a classic American car like a 1950s Cadillac in a funky colour like bubblegum pink! If the bride and groom are sports car fanatics, they could hire a spectacular set of wheels and roll up in a racy Ferrari, Porsche, Aston Martin – or even matching Mini Coopers à la Italian Job?
- Cabbing it – A white Hackney cab is an inexpensive, practical and very stylish way to be transported to the wedding.

- Pony (and trap) – Make the perfect fairy-tale wedding with a horse and carriage. Intensely romantic and very picturesque, this mode of transport is perfect for a country wedding where there are no busy roads.
- Chopper's away – For an entrance worthy of a Bond girl, arrival by helicopter is not only a thrilling way to travel, but it can also be very practical, especially if the ceremony venue is some way from the bride's home or the reception.
- Water berth – For a wedding in a riverside hotel, the bride could arrive by boat.
- Something on the side – For a cute and quirky means of transport, a vintage motorbike and sidecar would be perfect.

What are you wearing?

Traditionally, the best man, the father of the bride, ushers and pageboys all take their lead from the outfit chosen by the groom. If morning dress is to be hired, it's a good idea to try and arrange for all the fittings to be done together or at least by the same supplier.

How to look sharp

Together with the groom, decide on the outfits for both yourselves and the ushers to wear. It is usual for each person to pay for his own hire cost. If hiring morning dress, it is best to try to get everyone together for the fittings or at least ensure they all go to the same supplier. At the very least, phone round and make sure that all the men know what they're supposed to be wearing and from which shop. If the bridegroom is unable to collect the wedding outfits then this duty will also fall to you. Be sure to check that the outfits are complete and that nothing is missing. Don't forget to find out where the buttonholes for you and the groom will be on the wedding day – you'll need them before other guests do.

Wedding style

There are many styles for you and the groom to choose from. Have a look at some of the most popular options that follow.

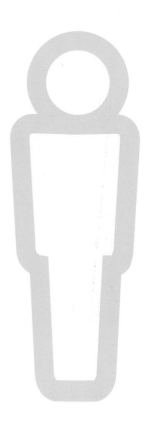

Morning dress

The morning suit (penguin suit, top hat and tails) is usually worn for weddings before 3pm, and is still the most popular attire. The cut and style of the coat is very flattering to the majority of figures, and consists of a blue, black or grey tailcoat paired with matching or contrasting trousers, either plain or pinstriped. The outfit is completed by a white wing-collar shirt, a waistcoat of any colour, a cravat, a top hat and gloves (just held, not worn!).

Black tie

Black tie is traditionally worn for weddings later in the day or for those to be followed by a formal reception, and is ideal for a grand evening reception or summer ball. A black dinner jacket, either single- or double-breasted, with ribbed silk lapels and no vents or covered buttons is worn. Trousers should be tapered, suitable for braces and, officially, have one row of braid. The evening shirt, in cotton or silk, with either a Marcella or a pleated front, has a soft, turn-down collar.

Accessories The bow tie is of black silk. Cummerbunds may be worn (with pleats opening upwards), but waistcoats are still much more acceptable. Black tie can be made as individual as you like with a colourful bow tie, matching waistcoat and pocket-handkerchief. Shoes should be black and well polished, and socks plain black.

White tie One step smarter than black tie is white tie. However, this is not usually worn for weddings.

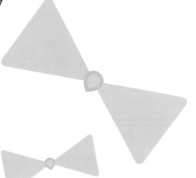

Frock coat

If you want to mark your wedding by wearing something different, a popular choice is the frock coat, which is available in many colours and fabric designs. Usually made in beautiful brocade (or plain velvet), it looks great paired with a pair of plain black trousers and a wing-collar shirt and cravat.

Lounge suit

The important thing at any event, and especially at a wedding, is to feel at ease. Lounge suits are a good alternative to more formal attire. This is definitely a sharp and sophisticated choice, and while associated with register office weddings, is perfectly acceptable for religious weddings as well.

Got the blues?

Many grooms in the armed forces choose to be married wearing their regimental uniform. The traditional uniform for weddings is the 'Blues' uniform: a blue jacket with a high collar, adorned with five brass buttons down the front and two on each cuff for officers. The jacket is teamed with matching blue trousers with a red stripe down the outside of each leg. No shirt is worn but the uniform is accessorized with a white belt and gloves. Military uniform can be worn by grooms who are full-time members of the armed forces.

Traditional outfit

The best-known and most popular of these is Highland morning or evening dress, traditionally worn by Scottish grooms. The kilt should be accompanied by a Bonnie Prince Charlie jacket or doublet, a sporran, laced brogues, socks, bow tie, and *sgian-dhu* (a small dagger carried in your sock).

Formal dress

Even if it's not a traditional wedding ceremony, whatever your culture or religion you can still wear either the appropriate full traditional outfit or adapt various aspects of it to personalize any formal dress.

Beach wedding

If the wedding is going to be on a beach or in a hot climate, there's a whole range of options available. In the linen suit department there's everything from Man from Del Monte/Pierce Brosnan chic to Miami Vice crushed casual style. Just remember, light shirts, no ties, Panama hats optional. Or how about a custom-made silk suit?

Overseas advice

If you want to smarten up your act a bit, a white tuxedo is great for overseas weddings in hot climates. A white jacket is best teamed with black trousers, a white pleated-front evening shirt and black bow tie.

Shoes

The choice of shoes is also personal, although the rule is not to wear brown shoes with black trousers and vice versa. A well-fitting pair of leather shoes is your best choice, regardless of how comfortable your old trainers are.

How to tie a tie

The Bow Tie

1 Start with A 4 cm (1½ in) below B.
2 Take A over then under B.
3 Double B in half and place across the collar points.
4 Hold B with thumb and finger; drop A over.
5 Pull A through a little, then double A and pass behind, then through the hole in front.
6 Poke resulting loop through; even it out, then tighten.

The Four-in-Hand

1 Start with A about 50 cm (20 in) below B.
2 Take A behind B.
3 Continue wrapping right round.
4 Pull A up through the loop.
5 Pull A down through loop in front.
6 Tighten.

   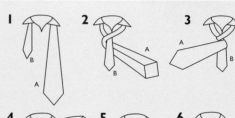

The Windsor

1 Start with A about 60 cm (24 in) below B.
2 Take A behind B and up through loop.
3 Bring A over and behind B.
4 Take A down through loop again.
5 Then over and up through loop.
6 Bring through the knot and tighten.

Pre-wedding checklist

Here's a handy list, summarizing the best man's traditional responsibilities during the run-up to the wedding day:

- Be involved in discussions and decisions in the planning stage with the groom, acting as a sounding board for his ideas.
- Help the groom choose the ushers, who are usually picked from both the bride and groom's families and friends.
- Make sure the ushers are aware of their responsibilities, that they attend fittings of outfits and are available to attend the rehearsal (if required).
- Together with the groom, decide on the outfits for both yourselves, and the ushers. If the outfits are hired, it is usual to expect each to pay for his own hire, unless the groom says otherwise.
- Prepare your speech well in advance.
- Attend the wedding rehearsal and check car-parking facilities and access, particularly if there will be disabled guests.
- Arrange the stag night to take place at least a few days before the wedding to give everyone enough time to recover from the celebrations.
- Collect any hire outfits if the bridegroom is unable to and check that the outfits are complete.
- Find out where you can collect buttonholes for yourself and the groom on the wedding day.

The
stag
night

Organizing the stag party

It's up to you to organize the stag night, the groom's traditional farewell to the single life. In preparing your send-off, resist the pressure to live up – or down – to the abundance of stag-night horror stories. Sure, you may want the groom to be the butt of a few jokes, but the stag night should ultimately be an affectionate celebration, rather than a gruesome ordeal of initiation. And today's stag dos are all about originality and style!

Traditionally, the groom is kept in the dark about his stag do, but it's probably a good idea to discuss with him what sort of celebration he wants. Get planning and get creative. First, you need to find out exactly who he wants to invite and compile a guest list. For example, does he want to include work colleagues and parents or just make it a smaller group of close friends? Think about the group's ages and interests – different activities throughout the day may need to be organized, for example, go-karting for all, after which parents and the younger contingent can leave while the big boys go clubbing.

Get the groom to give you the contact details for everyone he wants to invite and try to get in touch with everyone as soon as possible, to maximize the chances of everyone being free at the same time. Remember, this is your opportunity to really take charge and concoct a memorable event for the groom and the other guys in the party, so don't leave things to chance. You can make the difference between just another night in the pub and a legendary send-off – and no, it's not down to your karaoke performance of *My Way*.

When and where to hold the stag party

Nowadays, the night before the wedding is considered a definite no-no for the stag party. The best time is at least a week before the big day and, if possible, over the same weekend as the bride's hen party – this means the couple won't lose two weekends together in the crucial last few planning weeks before the wedding. You'll also need to think about the party location. Do most of your friends live in the same area, or is there a central town that's easily accessible for everyone?

Cash-wise, everyone generally pays for themselves and chips in to cover the groom too. It's less hassle to ask everyone to contribute towards a kitty before you go out. If you're spending a weekend away, send everyone a note or e-mail asking for a cheque in advance to cover their costs. Make it clear that unless they pay up you can't reserve their place.

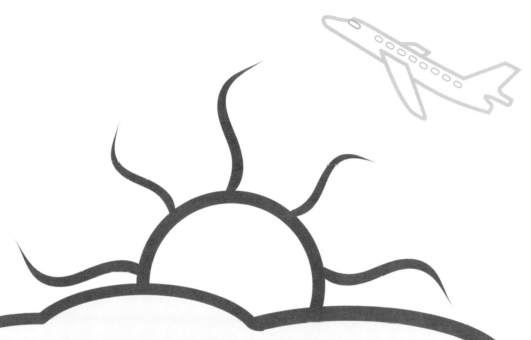

Joint hen and stag party

While still very much the non-traditional option, some couples opt to have a joint hen and stag party. They're usually best when the majority of the bride and groom's friends already know each other. If you are planning one, make sure it's not going to cause problems for couples with children who might have difficulty getting a babysitter.

Places to go

- Weekends abroad – with cheap flights everywhere, Paris, Brussels, Barcelona and Rome are hot destinations for hens and stags. You could try to time it around a local festival, exhibition or sporting event.
- Activity days – tank or sports car driving, paintballing and other outdoor activities are all great options for a memorable stag event.

On the day or night

It's your responsibility to look after the groom and make sure he returns home in one piece. The bride will know who to blame if he doesn't! Don't let the groom attempt to do anything or drink any more than he could normally cope with on a night out.

Your main challenge is to keep the momentum going, so try to pace the events. If lots of alcohol is involved, don't let everyone – especially not the groom! – drink too much too soon. Planning a meal in a restaurant as part of the celebrations or organizing food to be laid on in a pub will help with this.

And don't forget that it's the best man's job to make sure people don't play jokes on you or your groom that may not seem funny in the morning, such as dyeing his hair blue or sending him off on a cross-Channel ferry!

A sight for sore eyes

Take a camera with you to ensure the crimes of the memorable event are recorded, or a video camera to capture all the live action! Disposable cameras are available to buy at numerous shops and also on the Internet. For instance, see www.confetti.co.uk.

Paying up

The stag/hen costs should be divided among the group – you and the groom shouldn't have to pay for anything. If a pub crawl is planned, the money needs to be sorted out before people get too carried away – it's a good idea for everyone to be asked to contribute towards a kitty at the start of the evening. If it's an action day or weekend away that involves making a group booking, a note/e-mail can be sent in advance to everyone taking part asking for a cheque to cover costs. The best man or chief bridesmaid should make it clear that unless they pay up their places can't be reserved!

Top ideas

If you and the groom are not sure what sort of stag party to organize here's some of the questions to consider so that you start to get a clearer picture. Do you want to spend a weekend being active? Being creative or cultural? Do you want to be in the lap of luxury? Or would you prefer a traditional boozy weekend? Do you want to party close to home, or would a weekend away go down well? Maybe you want to go abroad for a stag weekend to really remember. Whatever you decide, here are some great ideas for activities to suit different groups.

For clubbers

If you want to rave the night away, bear in mind that many clubs have a strict door policy, so phone your chosen club in advance to check you're welcome – and ask if they offer group discounts. Alternatively, you could book a party bus tour of nightclubs in a big city such as Leeds or London: wine and beer on the bus, plus all entry fees are usually included in the price.

For daredevils

Adrenaline junkies could book up for a stag bungee jump, or take to the skies in a stunt plane to loop the loop and barrel roll! White-water rafting, trapezing above lakes and rivers on a zip wire or zooming about in a powerboat off the coast are great ideas for summer stags.

For action men

Organize a day of paintballing where you can team up and practise your SAS skills, or how about dry-slope skiing or snowboarding for a day's action. Or, if the budget is tight, organize a game of football or softball in a local park and follow it up by after-action pints in a favourite pub.

For boy racers

Take to the roads on an exhilarating driving stag: choose from a day at Brands Hatch pushing a Ferrari to its limits; tearing across rough terrain in a 4x4 or competing against your mates in a go-karting race.

For party animals

Pack your bags for a mad weekend of partying! The most popular places to head for include Amsterdam, Barcelona and Dublin. Get quotes from travel agents to give everyone a costing before they commit themselves. Once you've got a firm number, ask everyone for full payment before booking.

For modern couples

Some couples opt for a joint hen and stag celebration. If you have a big budget you might like to invite ten friends each to a country house for a weekend of horse-riding and playing ball! Alternatively, you and the chief bridesmaid could cook a meal at your home or hers and invite the happy couple and guests for dinner and silly board games.

For gamblers

Organize a night at the dogs or set up a mini casino at home. Specialist companies supply gaming tables, accessories, croupiers and funny money for an authentic touch! For an ultimate weekend of gambling, fly out to Las Vegas for the weekend. This is a 24-hour city with no 'last orders'!

Carry on camping

Borrow a couple of tents, jump into a camper van and head off to the seaside or the dales. Remember to take sausages, marshmallows and a guitar. Oh – and a torch.

For drinkers

Spice up a basic pub crawl by adding dares, getting your mates to each tell a relevant story about the groom in a different pub or playing pub golf. Or you could even make one of your stops a karaoke bar... Why not get together in a gang and set off to Blackpool or other seaside venue for a weekend of home-grown fun? Trawl along the promenade for slot machines and cheap and cheerful places to drink.

On course

Pick a top golf course like Valderrama, Gleneagles or La Manga, and organize your own Masters Championship. No need to carry your clubs here, just make sure you've got plenty of drinks stashed away in the buggy.

Chill out

Who says that stag weekends have to be about getting plastered? Why not go to a spa retreat or health farm? Book you and your mates in for a massage, to cleanse your mind and body so you'll be completely relaxed come the big day.

Stag night checklist

Don't let the logistics spoil your celebrations. To make sure everything goes well, have a definite plan and stick to it! Here's a handy list to help you remember what needs to be organized:

- Draw up a list of people to invite, in consultation with the groom.
- Select a town/venue that's easily accessible to everyone.
- Decide on what kind of stag party would be best for the people involved, establish an itinerary and make enquiries and then some provisional bookings.
- Pre-book everything you can so you're not thwarted by not being able to get into a venue/restaurant. Confirm bookings in writing (especially accommodation) and reconfirm the day before, too.
- Let invitees know well in advance if there's anything extra they should bring along with them – such as props, funny stories about the bride/groom, old photos, a change of clothes – and be contactable to answer any queries.
- Create and send out invitations.
- Make sure that everyone knows exactly where you're meeting. Give a contact number – ideally a mobile phone number – for any last-minute changes/confirmations.
- Make sure everyone knows roughly how much the do will cost – and that they'll be helping to cover the groom's costs. Let everyone know how and when payment should be made.
- Have a fall-back meeting place for late arrivals/people who get lost.
- Find out how everyone will get back home. Do you need to arrange transport/book taxis/send younger members of the party home earlier?

Duties
on
the big
day

The wedding morning

You will have a lot to do on the wedding day itself – so much, in fact, that you probably won't even have time to get nervous about your speech (as if...!). Prior to the ceremony, it's traditional to pop round to the bride's house to pick up buttonholes, telegrams, last-minute messages and any final instructions about seating arrangements, and so on.

On the wedding day

A best man's role on the wedding day is of the utmost importance. The groom will no doubt be very nervous and calm support is vital. The following pages explain in detail just what you need to do to ensure everything runs smoothly on the day...

- Meet the groom at least a couple of hours before you need to leave for the ceremony/venue and help ensure he looks his best.
- Check the groom has everything he will need for the honeymoon, especially the tickets and passports. Make sure you put the honeymoon luggage in the right vehicle.
- Collect the buttonholes for the groom, ushers and yourself.
- It is traditional to check with the bride about final arrangements and also any last-minute messages you might need.

Before setting off
Most importantly, make sure you have the ring(s) and money for the church fees (civil wedding fees will have been paid beforehand). A telephone call to the bride's father telling him when you are leaving will be welcome! Take the groom to the ceremony venue, making sure you arrive at least 30 minutes before the ceremony is due to begin. Check you have some confetti, but you should make sure that the venue allows it to be thrown.

Before the ceremony

As best man, you, of course, will have arrived at the church or register office early with the groom, giving yourself plenty of time to make sure things run as smoothly as possible. Check that you have the rings (again). Check that the order of service sheets have been brought to the venue to hand to guests as they arrive.

Make sure your ushers are wearing their buttonholes. If buttonholes have been ordered for guests, check they have been delivered to the venue. Get the ushers in line! Organize one on each side of the entrance to hand out order of service sheets. If the couple are following a traditional seating plan, make sure the ushers know to direct the bride's relatives to the left-hand side of the church and the groom's relatives to the right. If the bride and groom have a page-boy or ring bearer in the wedding party, have a chat, so he knows when he'll need to step up to the mark with the rings. Once you've reassured yourself that everything is in order, make your way to your appointed place alongside the groom.

At the ceremony venue

Whatever you are feeling inside, do not look nervous – the groom has enough on his mind. A few minutes before the bride's entrance and procession, you and the groom will stand to take your places at the front of the venue. (You are always to the groom's right.) Follow the service attentively, since your next job is the biggest of all: to produce the wedding ring(s) on cue for the groom.

The wedding ceremony

Church wedding

If the ceremony is in a church, you will need to:

- Pay the church fees on behalf of the groom and check one last time you've got those rings.
- Take your seat with the groom on the front right-hand pew while waiting for the bride. Shortly before the bride arrives, you will be prompted to stand in position at the head of the aisle, to the groom's right.
- Hand over the ring(s) at the right time during the ceremony – your big moment.
- After the service, accompany the chief bridesmaid (or matron of honour) and the bride and groom to the vestry for the signing of the register. You may also be asked by the groom to sign the register as a witness.
- Join the recessional down the aisle following in line after the bride and groom, the bride's father and groom's mother and the groom's father and the bride's mother. Escort the chief bridesmaid from the church on your left arm.

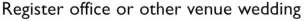

Register office or other venue wedding

Your role at the register office is very similar to that in a church. If there are no last-minute emergencies to attend to, then you can take up your position on the right of the groom. Here's what you need to do:

- You and the groom will be seated on the front right-hand seats while waiting for the bride to arrive. Shortly before the bride enters, you will be prompted to stand in position before the registrar.
- If the bride and groom have decided to exchange rings in the ceremony, be alert to the moment when you have to hand them over.
- You may be required to be one of the two witnesses who sign the register with the bride and groom at the end of the ceremony.

Post-ceremonial duties

Immediately after the ceremony, the best man has various duties to perform. You may have to help the photographer in rounding up guests for various group photographs if necessary. Ensure that all the guests have adequate directions and transport to the reception, arranging lifts where needed. You will need to do this promptly as you will be expected to leave for the reception venue with the bridesmaids immediately after the bride and groom so that you arrive shortly after.

The shoot list
The traditional group shots include:
- bride and groom with bride's family
- bride and groom with groom's family
- bride and groom with wedding party
- bride and groom with attendants

The other 'appearances', as they are known, should include:
- groom and best man outside the church/venue
- bride's arrival at the church/venue
- bride and father walking down the aisle/bride entering the venue
- bride and groom at the altar/desk
- exchange of rings
- signing of the register/documentation
- procession out of the church/venue
- group shots outside the church/venue
- arriving at the reception
- cutting the cake

However, a reportage style of photography is very much in vogue at the moment. You might also like to put a disposable camera on each of the tables at the reception.

Reception duties

When you get to the reception venue, your duties are as follows, though some will depend on whether you have agreed to take on the role of toastmaster:

- Collect any messages from the bride's father and check to see if any messages have been delivered directly to the reception venue.
- Join the receiving line, if asked to by the hosts, to greet and welcome guests as they move into the reception room and help them find their places.
- When everyone is seated and before the meal or buffet is served, call for silence and introduce the couple to the reception room as newlyweds.
- After the meal is finished, call for silence and introduce the speeches. Invite the bride's father to speak first (see page 47).
- After the bride's father has delivered his speech and toasted the bride and groom, introduce the groom for his much-awaited words! The groom's speech ends with a toast to the bridesmaids. You will reply to this toast on behalf of the bridesmaids, read congratulations from absent family and friends and deliver your speech (see pages 54–55), which should close by toasting the bride and groom.
- Once the speeches have concluded, you can breathe a sigh of relief and announce the cutting of the cake.

Stay focused

While it's easy to get completely absorbed in making your speech and forget about your other duties as best man, it's not in the interests of either your speech or your relationship with the groom to do so. Your role is a multiple one. Organizing the ushers, introducing guests to one another and generally making sure everything runs smoothly are all part of your job. If you concentrate on doing these things, you'll not only be fulfilling your role properly, but you'll also be distracting yourself from any pre-speech nerves.

Words of wisdom
Try not to worry about your role or responsibilities and let the pressure get to you – after all, the groom has chosen you because you're his best mate and he wouldn't have picked you if he didn't think you could do the job! Remember that it's not all about the ability to rattle off gags like a stand-up comedian. The best man has to be organized, must stay calm under pressure and also support the groom throughout the whole proceedings. So just relax, take it easy and retain your sense of humour at all times.

In accordance with tradition...

Of course you'll want to make your speech as entertaining as possible and as the groom's best friend, you will be expected to subject him to an ordeal of gentle embarrassment, but traditionally the best man's speech is also expected to fulfil certain functions. For instance, the best man will:

- Introduce all the other speakers, unless there is a toastmaster. Nowadays, speakers can be quite numerous as more people often choose to speak.
- Read out any messages from friends and family who haven't been able to attend and also pass on any practical announcements.
- Speak on behalf of the bridesmaids.
- Propose a toast to the bride and groom.

Last but not least

Speeches are traditionally given in a certain order:

- Father of the bride
- Groom
- Best man

It is more common nowadays for other people to make a speech, too – the mother of the bride and chief bridesmaid, for example, may also want to say a few words. But however many people speak, the best man traditionally always goes last – saving the best till then, hopefully.

Party time!

Once the big speech is out of the way you can relax a little.
It's tradition for the best man to dance with the chief
bridesmaid first, joining the bride and groom mid-way
through the first dance or for the second dance.

Your responsibilities are not over yet, however. You need
to keep a general eye on the proceedings. If wedding cameras
have been put out on the guests' tables, for example, ensure
they are used throughout the reception. Have fun decorating
the bride and groom's car – or whatever transport is taking
them away from the venue that evening. But make sure that
whatever you do, doesn't amount to criminal damage. The
happy – and hapless – couple will be relying on it, so bear
in mind that the car needs to remain in working order,
especially if they are going straight off on their honeymoon
and need to catch trains or flights later.

Finally, assist the hosts in bringing the celebrations to a
close, making sure everyone has transport home or can find
their room if they are staying overnight at the reception
venue. The hosts – especially if they are the bride and groom
– may appreciate it if you offer to check the bill and ensure
any outstanding payments are settled at the end of the night.
When you leave the venue, take a last look round for any
stray presents or lost property. Collect them together and
keep them safe until you can return them to their rightful
owners. As soon as possible after the wedding, arrange to
collect any hired outfits so that they can be returned and
deposits refunded. Make sure any items left at the venue find
their way back to their owners.

Checklist of duties on the day

If you have been organized in the months and weeks before the wedding day, everything should fall neatly into place and there shouldn't be any nasty surprises or last-minute emergencies. However, there is still a lot to remember and the best man will be the busiest member of the wedding party. Here's a checklist for the day:

- Collect buttonholes and any telegrams or other messages that will need to be read out at the reception.
- Check you have the rings.
- Make sure you have your speech notes with you!
- Arrange for the bride and groom's luggage to be stored for easy access later on.
- Make sure you have cash to pay relevant suppliers on the day and that you know exactly how much is owed to each supplier.
- Escort the groom to the ceremony venue, leaving plenty of time for the journey.

- Co-ordinate the ushers at the church or registry office, making sure they know where to sit people. Make sure the orders of service are to hand.
- Arrange buttonholes on yourself and the groom.
- Ensure all guests have directions and transport is arranged from the ceremony to the reception venue.
- Help the photographer get different groups together for the photographs.
- If you are acting as master of ceremonies as well, you will introduce the speeches and announce the cutting of the cake.

Writing your
speech

The best man's speech

People love wedding speeches – they look forward to them, listen to them, discuss them, remember them. The best man's speech is often the most eagerly anticipated and attentively listened to of all. So it's not surprising that making the speech has become the centrepiece of the best man's role and is likely to dominate the way in which you prepare for the big day. Before you get too stressed at the prospect, put your speech into perspective. True, you'll be the centre of attention for five minutes or so, but the day really belongs to the bride and groom, and most of the time everyone will be focusing on them. The trick is to make your five minutes really count. A best man's speech should be something that all the guests remember for the right reasons – because it's entertaining, funny, touching, considerate and does everything that it's supposed to. This might seem like a tall order if you're not practised in the art of public speaking, but with the right approach and lots of preparation you can do it.

Good timing

Speeches are usually made after the main meal, so by the time the best man comes to make his, the guests tend to have relaxed considerably (a fact not unconnected with the amount of wine consumed). This can often work in your favour, as by now, the guests will be nicely warmed up and well disposed to laugh at your jokes. However, this can also mean that you end up spending the meal feeling nervous – or worse, over-indulging in the name of Dutch courage. A drink or two may help steady your nerves, but make sure that you don't overdo it: a slurred speech will be remembered for all the wrong reasons!

How long should it be?

Timing is crucial when it comes to speeches. However brilliant yours is and however good a speaker you are, five minutes is more than enough. People enjoy listening to speeches, true, but they want to get on with talking and dancing, so keep it short. Rambling speeches are a mistake. Make sure yours has a clear beginning, middle and end. Avoid telling shaggy dog stories in favour of short, pithy jokes and asides. When it comes to speeches, less is definitely more.

Preparing your speech

Preparation is at the heart of a good speech. Scribbling down a few words the night before the big day is not going to work. Keep your speech on the back burner of your brain as soon as you know you are going to be best man, and start really working on it a few weeks before the wedding. It's an unfailing rule: the more prepared you are, the more confident you will be about giving your speech, and the more your audience will enjoy it. And the more you'll enjoy it, too.

What to include

Remember that your speech will be expected to include:

- Thanks to the groom for his toast on behalf of the bridesmaids and for any gifts that were presented.

- Comments on the bride and groom – you could mention how great they look today or why they're so compatible.
- Compliments to the groom. Brides always get a lot of the attention at weddings, and your speech is a good chance to redress the balance a little.
- Amusing anecdotes about the groom's past misdemeanours and/or a few jokes at the groom's expense.

Putting it all together

Decide what kind of speech you want to make before you start putting it together. There are various options. Traditionally the best man makes the speech solo, but nowadays it's not unusual to make a joint speech with the ushers, other friends or the chief bridesmaid. You can consider performing a stunt with the aid of a few props, or you may want to use a home video or slides or invent funny telegrams. Adopt a well-known format to comic effect. For example, you could write a mock school report for the bride/groom and base your jokes around that.

Don't think about your speech as one big lump. Break it down into headings and decide what you're going to say under each one – for instance, how you met the groom, how the bride and groom got to know each other, the wedding preparations. Then look at all the elements and work out the best order to fit them together.

Tips for success

These tips will help you as you begin to prepare your speech:

- Use a notebook so you can jot down ideas as they occur to you.
- A tape recorder will enable you to practise and time your speech.
- Ask friends and family to listen to your speech and give you feedback and ideas.
- Think about what props will work most effectively with your chosen theme.
- Carry a copy of the latest draft of your speech with you, so you can make notes and work on it whenever you have a spare moment.

The right material

Wedding speakers have it tough. Who else has to make a speech that will appeal to an audience with an age range of 2 to 82? Speeches have to make people laugh without offending anyone's sensibilities, talk about families and relationships without treading on anyone's toes and hold people's attention without stealing the show from the happy couple. It sounds like a tall order, but most of the pitfalls of speech-making can be avoided if you know what to talk about and recognize that there are limits around certain subjects. It's all a matter of choosing and using your material with care.

Definite no-nos
You can get away with talking about a lot of subjects, provided you're genuinely witty and don't cross the line into bad taste. Some things, however, are absolutely off-limits. Steer clear of these topics:

- Race
- Religion
- Ex-partners
- People who refused to attend
- Last-minute threats to call off the wedding
- Swearing
- Explicit sexual references

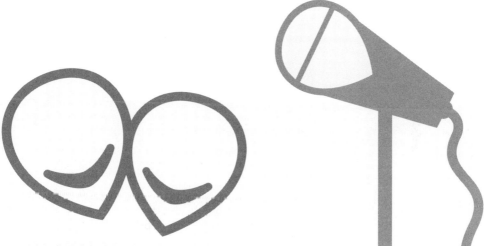

Keep it positive

Weddings aren't the place for criticism. Don't knock anything relating to the venue or the service, and don't make jokes at other people's expense, especially the bride's. This is the happy couple's perfect day and you need to help keep it that way by considering other people's feelings at all times.

The bride It's possible that you may have ambivalent feelings about the bride. Keep these firmly under wraps at the wedding.

Don't make any jokey remarks about her diet either! Compliments to the bride are the only permissible references to her in your speech.

Be kind Sure, your speech is about teasing the groom, but mix the mockery with some sincerity. Talk about how highly you think of him, what a good friend he is and how his relationship with the bride has enriched him. Give the couple all your very best wishes for the future.

Tailored to fit The material that you decide is suitable for your speech will depend on your audience. It's up to you to find out who you'll be talking to, and to check beforehand that what you're planning to say won't cause offence. If you can rehearse your speech in front of your mum and granny without you or them feeling at all uncomfortable, then you've got the tone right.

Do your research

Good research can turn a mildly amusing speech into an uproariously funny one. Nothing can beat that cringe-inducing anecdote or photo from the groom's early years, which you've managed to excavate and which he was clearly hoping no one could possibly remember – and may even have forgotten about himself. As best man you probably know the groom very well, but you may not know much about his family life or early schooldays – times people enjoy hearing anecdotes from. So start your research early so that you have time to gather everything you need.

Friends united

The best sources of stories about a bride and groom are, of course, their friends and family. Siblings, cousins and colleagues usually have some great anecdotes to tell. As soon as you know you're doing a speech, send out e-mails asking people who know the couple for any funny/touching stories they think you could include. Or invite everyone out for a drink, bring your tape recorder along and let them reminisce away. You're sure to come away with some great material.

Every picture tells a story

Photograph albums are a great source of speech material, too. Old pictures, or the stories behind them, can be hilarious. If there's a snap of the groom or bride pulling a face in a school photo or looking cute as a toddler, get it blown up to display on the night and work it into the speech.

For example, a picture of the groom as a five-year-old enjoying a donkey ride at the seaside can be used as an illustration of his lifelong affection for the gee-gees, while a snap of him as a naked tot in the bath can show how much he's always loved water sports. Not everyone at the wedding may have known the bride and groom for long. Using photographs of them as tiny children can help to bridge the gap between friends and family. It also gives you licence to comment on their childhood hobbies, eccentricities, fashion sense, etc. and make comical comparisons with the grown-up people they are today.

What the papers say

Are there any newspaper cuttings about the bride and groom? Perhaps he appeared in the local paper in his days as top goal scorer for the under-nines football team, or she was a prize-winning Girl Guide. You could use this type of material to illustrate how much they've changed... or how much they haven't, as the case may be.

You could also look at the news for the year the groom was born and work it into your speech. For example: '1969 was the year Neil Armstrong took a small step for man and a giant leap for mankind by walking on the moon, and coincidentally, it was also the year Paul took his first steps...'

If you can find a photograph of the groom taking his first steps to accompany your speech, so much the better.

Revealing sources

There's often mileage in the meaning of the names of the bride or groom. For example:

'Apparently, the name Gary means "spear carrier". Well, I don't know about a spear but he certainly carries a torch for Kathleen.'

You could also compare the meanings of the couple's names.

Whatever they like

You don't have to stick to jokes about football teams – hobbies and interests of all kinds can form the basis of lots of stories. However, you might not be as familiar with the groom's object of obsession as he is. In this case, the Internet is a great source of information. If one of the happy couple is a huge fan of any singer or celebrity and their obsession is well known, you could use it in your speech. For example:

'Roger has always been a major Elvis fan, and when he met Rachel he was certainly All Shook Up. He almost moved into Heartbreak Hotel when he thought she wasn't interested...'

Tips for success

Computers can be used to great effect to create front page newspaper mock-ups: you could use a *Sun* headline such as 'Gotcha' to accompany a picture of the couple getting engaged. Get the picture blown up as large as possible and display it while you're making your speech.

Make it work

Working life and old bosses can be a source of great material. If you're not a colleague of the bride or groom, get in touch with their workmates past and present and ask them for any good office anecdotes. Just make sure that everyone will understand them.

Academic archive

Old schoolbooks, school reports and university notes can also provide material. Ask one of the groom's family to get them down from the attic and take a look. If there's a school report saying how your high-flying friend and groom will never amount to a hill of beans, or a funny essay they wrote when they were ten, it could be amusing to read it out.

The do's and don'ts of speech-writing

Past loves

There's nothing wrong with talking about the groom's previous loves – provided they are firmly in the far distant past. Tell guests about the flirtation he had with that cute little blonde... in the sandpit back at nursery school. Don't tell them about the girl who broke his heart when he was 16 and whom he's never really forgotten – or about any other romance he's had since the age of seven, for that matter. It's also worth noting that while you can make vague allusions to the groom's sowing of wild oats – such as 'He was a bit of a wild lad at college' – you should never even hint at anything similar about the bride. Double standards still apply, at least at weddings!

The happy couple's relationship

Comments about the bride and groom are usually part of the best man's speech. Tread carefully, however, especially if their relationship has been stormy in the past. Tell guests about how their first meeting generated enough electricity to power the National Grid. Talk about how compatible they are and how great they both look today. Don't tell them about how they slept together within half-an-hour of meeting or about how she left him for someone else for six months. Arguments, estrangements and threats to call off the wedding are all off limits. If in any doubt, leave it out.

Great gags: the key game

This is a favourite among wedding speech-makers as it really helps to break the ice. To play it, you need to speak to all the female guests beforehand (you might have to hang around the ladies at the reception to do it) and fill them in on the plan. It works like this – during your speech you say something like: 'Neil has got what you might call a chequered past, but now that he's married to Hannah it's time that he made a fresh start. So I'm asking any of his ex-girlfriends who may be present today to give back the keys to his flat. Just come up here and put them in this bowl. Come on girls, don't be shy.' Then, you've guessed it – all the women at the reception, from the groom's 90-year-old auntie to his four-year-old cousin come up to put a set of keys in the bowl. It's guaranteed to get laughs and helps everyone to relax.

Family matters

Complimenting the bride and groom's families can be part of your speech – but make sure you stick to compliments only. Tell guests how your best friend, the groom, has wonderful parents – and now he's gaining great parents-in-law, as well as a lovely wife. Or congratulate the bride's parents for organizing the wedding so well. Don't tell them how you're amazed to see the groom's father there at all since he walked out on the family when the groom was still in his pram. Speeches shouldn't be used for settling scores. Avoid comments about divorced or warring parents. If the family situation is very sensitive, don't make the mistake of thinking you can make things better with a few carefully chosen lines.

Great gags: loud and clear
A quick visual gag can get a speech off to a good start. For example, you could begin speaking to the audience but mumble so much that they can't hear a word you're saying. You can then produce a huge loudhailer and roar, 'Can you hear me at the back?' through it. This will soon get the audience's attention!

The wedding

Behind-the-scenes stories about preparing for the wedding, especially amusing incidents and narrowly averted disasters, make good ingredients for speeches. However, you might be surprised at how sensitive these subjects can be. Very few families exist who don't have the odd squabble over wedding arrangements. Sometimes these disagreements seem amusing by the time the big day arrives – but sometimes they are still sore points, so take care. Tell guests how fantastically the day has turned out and how it's all down to the hard work of the organizers. Don't tell them about how the bride's mother almost had a nervous breakdown over the seating plan – unless you're absolutely sure she'll think it's funny. As always, run your speech by someone close to the family.

Read the signs

Introduce your speech by saying that you've got a sore throat and can't speak very loudly, so your friend is going to use sign language to interpret what you're saying. Your friend will then make amusing, exaggerated and ridiculous hand gestures to accompany your speech. Obviously, this one will need quite a lot of rehearsal.

Bit of a lad

People expect to hear funny stories about the groom's misdemeanours as part of the best man's speech. Joshing him gently is all part of the fun, but do make sure that your anecdotes are humorous rather than offensive. Tell guests about the time he redecorated the living room with crayon when he was a little lad. Don't mention how he was all over that lap dancer at his stag night, then vomited copiously in the minicab all the way home. Keep quiet about criminal records, expulsions from school and the like, too.

In-jokes

Making everyone feel included is a key element in the best man's speech, so bear this in mind when you're writing it. You need to explain references that not everyone may be familiar with, and if this takes too long, it's much better to think of another anecdote. Tell guests about how, one year, the groom broke three-dozen eggs in the school egg and spoon race. Don't bother bringing up the hilarious time in metalwork when the groom got told off by that mad Mr Smith, you know, the metalwork teacher, he was really mad, and he sent him to see Miss Green, the one who all the lads fancied... you really had to be there.

Picture perfect

Why not bring along a flip chart with photographs and a pointer to help liven up your speech? The pictures don't have to be ones of the happy couple as toddlers or newspaper cuttings of their achievements. Instead there could be a skip, representing the groom's first car; a picture of a bombsite, representing his bedroom and so on. It's a simple idea, but can get big laughs.

Great gags: mopping up

Here's an example of another visual gag. Harry and Sam are a pair of brothers known for their sensitivity, so when Harry got married it wasn't surprising that both he and best man Sam were in floods of tears before the speeches had even began. But when the time came for Harry to be Sam's best man, he decided to come prepared. Before beginning his speech, he produced an enormous plastic bag stuffed with packets of tissues, which he distributed among the audience. It wasn't long before they were throwing them back at him.

Hands-on help

If you're worried about any aspect of your speech, talk to someone who's been there before. Talking to someone with experience will calm your nerves and give your confidence a boost. If they still have a copy of their speech, ask to see it. They can advise on how to source material, where they got their ideas from and how they put everything together. You can also learn from their mistakes, rather than making your own. They may have unwittingly stumbled on a sensitive subject, or their speech may have overrun or been too short. Ask them what really worked and what could have been improved on. Finding out what not to do can be a great help in making your own effort a success. Ask them to look over your speech for some last-minute expert advice.

Using a Pro

Speech writing doesn't come naturally to everyone. Rather than spending months racking your brains for witty one-liners, you could turn to the professionals for help. This has become a popular option in recent years.

- There are many services available, ranging from general speeches you can adapt, to personalized speeches written for you.
- A speech-writer will work on your notes to ensure that the content relates to the groom and the tone suits your audience. Some writers provide cue cards to use.
- Be careful if you buy an 'off the peg' speech, they're cheaper but lack a personal element. It may appear clumsy if you try to insert the odd mention of the groom.
- Expect to pay anything from £20 to £30 for a general best man speech. A tailor-made speech can cost hundreds of pounds.
- The Internet and wedding magazines are good places to start your search for a good speech-writer.

Delivery

Your speech comes last, so you are going to spend some of the reception waiting to 'go on'. How you fill your time will affect your delivery.

Top tips

Don't overindulge Although it's very tempting to down a few too many glasses while you're waiting to speak – don't. Being tipsy could affect your delivery by making you slur your words and cause you to become unsteady on your feet. Too many drinks might also affect your judgement – you may decide that the risqué story about the groom's antics at the rugby club night out, which you deleted from your original speech, really should be in there after all.

Listen and learn Listening to the other speeches will help to take your mind off your nerves and put you into a fun mood. Having a few laughs will relax you and make the time pass more quickly until, before you know it, it's your turn.

Have a banana Many professional performers swear by eating a banana about 20 minutes before they are due to start speaking. Doing this, they say, will give you a quick energy boost and also help steady your nerves.

Cue best man

Start right
Don't try to begin your speech when there are lots of distractions. Wait until the audience has stopped applauding the previous speaker, the tables have been cleared, the coffee poured and everyone has settled down – then you will have people's undivided attention.

All in the mind
Instead of seeing your speech as a formal ordeal, think of it as being a conversation between you and a lot of people you know and really like, or as a way of wishing two good friends well. Thinking positively about your speech and the reason why you are there will help you to deliver it with confidence and make the task seem less intimidating.

To help calm your nerves beforehand, imagine your speech being over and everyone applauding. Imagine how you'll feel when you can sit down and relax, knowing that you've done your best and you can now really enjoy the rest of the evening. By visualizing everything going well, this will help to give you even more confidence.

They're on your side

Remember that weddings are happy occasions and all the guests want to see everything go well, including your speech. Be assured, the audience is on your side, they're all rooting for you, so make the most of it and use their goodwill to boost your confidence.

Stage fright

It's only natural to be nervous. If you find that you're really scared when you begin, don't panic. Make a joke out of it instead. Lines like 'This speech is brought to you in association with Imodium' or 'I was intending to speak but my tongue seems to be welded to the roof of my mouth', should raise a laugh and will help to get the audience on your side. One completely bald best man started off on a high note by remarking: 'As you can see, I've been so worried about making this speech, I've been tearing my hair out.' There's no shame in admitting you're a little bit scared.

Ten steps to a perfect speech

1 Eye to eye

Make eye contact when you're giving your speech – just not with everyone at once! Speak as if you were talking to one person and focus on them. You can look around the room if you want to, but focus on one person at a time. The trick is to imagine that you're simply chatting to someone.

2 Don't look down

Even if you decide to learn your speech off by heart, you will need to have some notes to refer to in case your mind goes blank in the heat of the moment. However, don't deliver your speech while hiding behind a quivering piece of paper or constantly staring downwards. Look down for a moment, look up and speak. Get into a rhythm of doing this throughout your speech.

3 No mumbling

When people are nervous, they tend to swallow their words;
this can render a beautifully written speech nearly inaudible.
You don't want to deliver your speech only to find that no
one could actually hear what you were saying, so check that
you're audible by arranging beforehand for someone at the
back of the room to signal when your voice isn't carrying

4 Breathtaking

Another way to combat the mumbling menace is by
breathing properly. Take deep, rhythmic breaths. This will
pump oxygen into your blood and helps to keep your brain
sharp and alert.

5 Set the pace

Gabbling is another thing people tend to do when they're
nervous. To stop yourself talking too fast, write the word
'pause' at intervals through your notes, or if you are using
cue cards, insert blank ones that will automatically cause you
to slow down. If you do happen to lose your place, it's best
just to make a joke of it.

6 Move on swiftly

Pause briefly after you make a joke to give people a chance
to laugh, but keep jokes and anecdotes short so that if one
doesn't work, you can move on quickly to the next. If your
joke dies, don't despair. Turn the situation to your advantage
by inserting a quip such as 'Only me on that one then', or
look round at an imaginary assistant and say: 'Start the car!'
'Rescue lines' like these can earn you a chuckle from a
momentarily awkward silence.

7 Keep smiling

Being best man and making a speech are supposed to be fun,
so make sure you don't look utterly miserable when you're
doing it. Smile! Think of something that makes you laugh
before you start speaking to get yourself into a light-hearted
mood. Body language is important, too, so adopt a relaxed
posture before you begin – no crossed arms or fidgeting.

8 Start strongly

Opening lines are important, because they grab the
audience's attention and get you off to a good start.
Something like: 'Ladies and gentlemen, they say speeches are
meant to be short and sweet, so thank you and good night,'
should help you to begin in style.

9 Give it meaning

Think about the meaning of your speech while you're making it. Concentrate on the thoughts you want to convey and the message behind your words, rather than simply reciting your notes, as this will help you to make the delivery of your speech much more expressive.

10 Round it off

End your speech with a toast. This will give it a focus and provide something to work towards. After you make your toast, you can sit down when everyone else sits down, signifying a definite end to your speech. Our range of sample toasts starts on page 148.

Prompts and props

Proper props

Physical gags, games, visuals and tricks can all be part of a best man's speech. So if you don't want to just read from a prepared text – let your imagination run wild. If your speech is going to involve the use of props, make sure that you do plenty of rehearsing with them, and also ensure that any machinery is in good working order before the big day.

Make 'em look

Simple props can be used to begin with a bang. One best man, for instance, started off his speech with the remark: 'I hate it when people use cheap gimmicks to get attention, don't you?' before whipping off his baseball cap and ponytail to reveal a completely bald pate.

Lots of different props can be used for this type of joke. Why not try:
- A revolving bow tie
- Clown feet
- A whistle
- A clown nose?

Instant nostalgia

Props don't have to be used only for jokes. You could put together video, photographs and newspaper cuttings to make a quick 'this is your life' of the bride and groom, or have a blast from the past by playing a tape of the band the groom used to be in. As with speeches, so with props – you should never attempt to wing it when making a speech and this is even more important when using props. Make sure that you rehearse well and run your ideas by other members of the wedding party to reduce the risk of your jokes falling flat.

Simple props

Hat trick
Have a series of funny hats under the table, which you put on as you run through the groom's life story – for example: a baby bonnet, a school cap, a mortar board, a fireman's helmet, a baseball cap, a deerstalker. The more ridiculous the hats are, the better.

Good report
Write a mock school report on the bride or groom and read it out, relating it to the events of the day, such as:

'It says here that Paula doesn't suffer fools gladly... which is bad news as she's just got married to Steve.'

Video diary
Get your friends together and make a spoof video documentary featuring their thoughts and feelings about the happy couple. Two of the guests could dress up as the bride and groom and re-enact their first meeting.

Pass the parcel
Present the bride with an enormous parcel. As she unwraps it, it gets smaller and smaller until she comes to a little box. In it, there's a note saying, 'I haven't got much to say, but thanks for padding out my speech.'

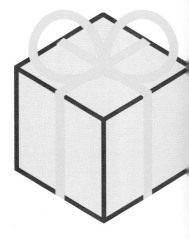

Ask the audience to play

Playing speech games is a great way of getting the whole audience to join in the fun. Here are some ideas to try:

The singing game Ask friends and family to help compile a list of words that describe the guests at each table. Put the lists on the respective tables and ask everyone sitting at them to make up a song or poem using all of the words on the list. They then have to stand up and perform it!

The limerick game This is another word game that everyone can enjoy. You put a note on all of the tables asking the guests to make up a short poem or a limerick about the couple. You can read out the best ones during your speech, or ask the guests to read out their own. Make it clear, however, that you don't want anything offensive.

The sweepstake game At the beginning of the reception, get the ushers to ask the guests to bet on the length of the speeches. The person who makes the closest guess wins the total amount, either to keep or to donate to a charity of their choice.

Final words on your speech

So you've done the research, gathered all your anecdotes and written one hell of a speech and/or toast. You've made sure that it contains all of the formal stuff, with a healthy dose of (not too) irreverent stories about the groom. Maybe there's a few sentimental words in there about how honoured you are to have been chosen as best man or how much the groom means to you as a mate. And, of course, you've included some suitable compliments about the bride. All you need to do now is get up there and give the speech. But before doing that, here are some final words of advice to make sure you do the best job possible on the big day.

Practise, practise, practise

'The more I practise,' said golfing legend Gary Player, 'the luckier I get.' Ask Tiger Woods or David Beckham how they became the best in their professions and they'll tell you it's all down to practise. Whatever your levels of confidence and competence about making the speech, putting time into your preparation will reap serious improvements. Use your partner, family and close friends as guinea pigs, running through the whole thing with them at least a couple of times. This will give you a chance to iron out any wrinkles in the text, hone the delivery of your punchlines and also change anything that really doesn't work.

Remember whose day it is

You're not the star of the show – the bride and groom are. Remember that, as best man, you are playing a supporting role, not taking centre stage. Obviously you want to entertain people, but not at the expense of the bride and groom and their enjoyment of the day.

Don't get drunk

For many people, having a few drinks when nervous is a way of relaxing and calming the nerves. Try and resist that temptation at all costs. One glass too many will only diminish your judgement and you could find yourself telling an offensive joke without realizing what you're doing. Reward yourself with a drink – after the speech.

Keep to the script

Ideally you'll have put your speech – if not verbatim, then in note form – on to prompt cards. Use them to keep your speech flowing and to make sure that you don't miss anything important out. But equally important, make sure you don't start adding things in. If the speech is going well, your confidence will soar and you may think that you should spice up a perfectly good, well-rehearsed speech with additional material. Unless you are a really experienced performer, stick to what you've practised.

Don't panic

No one knows what you're going to say in your speech. So if, for whatever reason, you skip a section, lose your place or simply dry up, don't worry. Most people won't know that you've gone wrong. Simply pause, find a place where you can get back on track and carry on from there.

Speak up, slow down

No matter how good your material is or how well you've rehearsed your gags, if the audience can't hear you, they are not going to laugh. The most common mistakes a best man can make are to mumble his words, talk to the floor or give the speech at a million miles an hour. Speak up and slow down, and you'll be fine.

Never heckle hecklers

When the nerves are jangling and the adrenaline is pumping, being interrupted by someone in the crowd can seem like the rudest thing you've ever heard in your life. You may be sorely tempted to tell the clever dick to keep their thoughts to themselves. Don't. If you get heckled, roll with it. Some people like to join in with the speeches at weddings and they almost certainly don't mean any harm. More often than not, the things people shout out are very funny. Laugh along with them and you'll find it helps you to relax.

And finally...

Think of your speech as a gift to your friends. It's an honour to have been asked, so see your words as a token of your appreciation, as well as your own contribution to their special day. Above all, enjoy yourself. If you are having a good time and speaking with goodwill, your audience cannot fail to warm to you.

Wedding speech checklist

No matter how much warning you've had of your best mate's upcoming nuptials and your role on the big day, the success of your speech will ultimately result from the amount of preparation you've put in. So as soon as you accept the job of best man...

- Start thinking about research.
- Think about the audience. Your speech will have to appeal to a wide range of people, from great aunt Nora to your friends from work. Find out who'll be among the guests so that your material appeals and you don't cause offence.
- Ask friends and family for funny stories/embarrassing pictures that you can build into your speech.
- Keep your speech in the back of your mind. You never know when you might pick up a titbit of information or some juicy material.
- Keep a notebook to hand. Great ideas often strike when you least expect them (like on the train or in the bath!).
- Speak to someone who's been a best man and find out what not to do.
- Decide on the kind of speech you want to make. Are you going to use any props, visual aids or equipment?

Countdown to your speech

The build-up

A few weeks before the big day, start working on your speech in earnest.

- Think about structure. Would the speech be better broken down into manageable chunks/themes?
- Does your speech do what it's supposed to do? Is it funny, affectionate and charming without being offensive to any members of the audience?
- Have you included everything you need to in your speech? Thanks to the groom for his toast to the bridesmaids, thanks to the organizers, etc.
- Find out who else will be making a speech. Nowadays the list of people who want to say a few words can be quite long and, unless there is a toastmaster, it will fall to you to introduce all the other speakers.
- Gather all the props/presentation aids you'll need and make sure you know how to use them.
- Build in time to practise your speech – the better rehearsed you are, the more confident you'll be, and the more everyone will enjoy it, yourself included.

Only a week to go

A week or so before the big day, start honing down your speech using the following tips.

- Use a tape recorder or video to record yourself.
- Rope in an audience of friends to practise on.
- Be sure to practise your speech with any props you plan to use – winging it on the day is not a good idea.
- Time your speech. Aim to keep it to around five minutes. Brevity really is the soul of wit.
- Don't forget to allow time for reading out messages from absent friends and family, passing on any practical announcements and so on.
- Write your speech in note form on cue cards, even if you intend to commit it to memory.
- Think positively about your speech and it will feel like less of an ordeal.
- Visualize your speech being over and everyone applauding as it will help to give you confidence and calm your nerves.
- Remember the audience is on your side – you'll be able to use their goodwill to boost your confidence.

Jokes
and one-liners

Make them laugh

Stuck for a witticism to fill out your epic speech? Looking for a rib-tickler or two to break up the serious or romantic bits with a chortle? Then let our directory of jokes and one-liners, based on real wedding speeches and toasts, take the strain. We've included all the subjects that most commonly come up in a wedding speech – everything from first impressions to the groom's sporting prowess. All you need to do is search for the subject you're after, or if you're stuck for inspiration, just dip in and browse. Not every line will fit the speech or toast you're planning exactly, of course, but hopefully you'll find an idea you can adapt, a line you can make your own. As you prepare your words, remember not to try too hard. You don't have to be a stand-up comedian to go down a storm at a wedding, just someone who's put a little time, care and thought into your speech.

How to be funny

Every speaker wants to raise the roof – or at least a few smiles. Don't feel under pressure to be funny. Remember that everyone's on your side and they want your words to work as much as you do.

- **Establish a rapport with your audience** Refer to something topical that everyone can relate to: 'Phew! I don't know about you but I thought I was going to keel over in that church...'

- **Nervous?** Don't panic. Make a gag about Imodium or jelly legs! (See pages 95.)

- **Enjoy yourself** Or at least try to look as if you are. It'll relax the room.

- **Keep it simple** If you have to explain the gag, you're doing it wrong!

- **Practice makes perfect** Test out your speech on friends and colleagues, note their reactions and amend as necessary.

- **Think of your whole audience** Avoid private in-jokes, technical jargon and anything offensive.

- **Be sensitive** Avoid referring to previous partners, weight problems, but if you have to, do so with great care. Above all, don't offend the bride. If in doubt, leave it out!

- **Be brief** Even the best speech can become a bit of a yawn if it goes on for too long.

- **Jokes aren't everything** Sometimes a few words spoken from the heart can be just as effective.

What the experts say

'The more you practise delivering your speech, the less nervous you will be. Practise the pauses, the intonations, the anecdotes. By showing you've put even a little thought and effort into what you're saying, all manner of sins will be forgiven. Recite your speech in the shower, on the bus, on the loo. On the night, your nerves will thank you, because instead of fretting about your audience or your flies, you'll simply focus on what you're going to say.'

Rob Pointer, stand-up comic and serial best man

'Don't speak when you're looking down at your notes. Look down for a moment, look up, smile at everyone, speak – then repeat. You don't need to talk constantly; it gives guests a break, and if you're not afraid of silence, you'll look confident, so everyone can relax. Remember that in between speaking, silence feels approximately ten times longer than it is, so take it nice and slow.'

Jill Edwards, comedy coach and scriptwriter

The good, the bad and the ugly

Lines that work

'I'm going to make this short and sweet. Thanks very much.' (Speaker sits down.)

'And so without further ado, let's raise our glasses...'

...and lines that don't

'I wouldn't say the bride looks fat in that dress, but...'

'Turning now to Simon's third marriage...'

'Not being a big fan of marriage myself...'

'When I was going out with the bride...'

Good for a groan

'Unaccustomed as I am to public speaking...'

Definite no-nos
- Any reference to bridal pregnancy (except by prior agreement).
- References to the cost of the wedding.
- References to any family feuds or tension.

Opening and closing lines

(At start of speech) 'And so, ladies and gentleman, will you please charge your glasses, and rise and join me... in the pub next door. This speech lark is far too pressurized: I'm going for a pint.'

'I've been told the essence of a good speech is to stand up and be seen, speak up and be heard, and sit down and shut up.' **(Sit down)**

'And, finally, I'd like to finish with a big thank you to all of those who managed to stay awake during my speech and even to laugh politely in one or two places. In fact, you've been such a lovely audience I only wish I'd had better material...'

Public speaking

'Unaccustomed as I am to pubic spanking... er... to public spending... er... to public speaking...'

(Adopt northern accent of old-style comic) 'Now here's another one you won't get: Why does a cucumber make a better lover than the mother-in-law? (Pause) 'Oh sorry. Wrong gig.'

Upstanding...

'And so, without further ado, let me ask those of you who still can to stand up and join me in a toast...'

'And so will everyone now please raise their glasses – and themselves...'

'And so, in the words of my ex-girlfriend, "I'm going to leave you now."'

Wedding guests

Absent guests/gatecrashers

'It's a great shame Colin couldn't be with us tonight, though I know a couple of people – Jack and Jim – who're quite glad he's not, as he always really lays into one of them. Mr Jack Daniels and Mr Jim Beam, that is.'

'It'll be easy to spot any gatecrashers today: they'll be the ones laughing at the jokes in my speech!'

Ushers

'If anyone needs assistance at all today, please don't hesitate to call an usher. You can't miss them: they're the ones wearing caps and holding torches...'

Zzzzz...

(Perhaps point at someone who looks like they are a likely candidate for dozing off)

'Of course, in certain cultures it's considered a compliment when a respected guest dozes off during your speech. (Pull out an enormous bullhorn, gong, bell or similar.) But I don't think that we'll have that problem here, do you?'

Best man

'I'm told that one of the few acceptable reasons for turning down the job of best man is when you don't know the groom that well and are not even really sure why you've been asked. Well nothing could be further from the case with me and Eric... I mean, Bert... I mean Steve...'

'They say that when it comes to the best man's speech the guests are usually nice and warmed up by all the booze and the sentimental speeches that have gone before. I just hope it doesn't get so warm that it brings the tumbleweed out...'

Nerves

'I'd like to say a big thank you to Alka Seltzer and Imodium, my speech co-sponsors.'

'Does anyone mind if I do this sitting down? Only my legs appear to have turned to jelly.'

'Normally I'm a terrible public speaker, but I'm so proud to see my son/daughter/best friend/brother get married today that I can barely summon a single nerve!'

Bride and groom

Aaaaagh!

'Tall, handsome, sensitive, intelligent, funny, brave, musical and athletic. I am all these things – so why on earth did Paula have to go and marry Mark?'

First boyfriend/girlfriend

'Dan's first girlfriend, when he was seven, was called Sarah. Her dad, Mr Taylor, used to run the clock shop up the road, so Dan's family called her Sarah "Tick Tock" Taylor. Unfortunately, she fell out with him when he tried to bribe her with a pencil sharpener to see up her skirt. They've not seen each other for 20 years, but tonight, ladies and gentlemen, thanks to the power of the Internet, HERE SHE IS... [make a big gesture and point to the nearest door, as if she's about to walk in, then pause, as nothing happens] No, not really.'

'It's not the done thing to say too much about exes in a wedding speech, I know, but I think that we should all spare a thought for Jane's former boyfriend Robbie. Robbie and Jane used to be inseparable. They'd go out for long cycle rides together, drink from the same straw, hold hands in the park. But, unfortunately, they split up over a tragic incident in which Robbie spilt paint over Jane's favourite outfit. She was the only girl in her class to have dungarees, and in all my life I've never seen a seven-year-old girl quite so upset.'

Handsome

'The groom didn't always look as good as he does today. When he was born the midwife took one look at him and slapped his father. His mum pushed the only pram in town with shutters. She used a catapult to feed him!'

Honeymoon

'Jake likes to unwind on holiday, but I hope he won't get too relaxed on his honeymoon with Jill. I know, from the rugby tours I've been on with him, that his idea of "relaxing" is not getting out of the bath to pee.'

Newlyweds

'I'm sure I speak for everyone when I say how much we wish Penny and Tim a long and happy future together, although I'm not sure it's a good sign that she keeps going round introducing Tim as "my first husband".'

'In the words of Groucho Marx, "Marriage is a wonderful institution, but who wants to live in an institution?"'

Romance

'I like to say that Liz and Mike were destined for one another. When they met, she was an occupational therapist specializing in mental health and he... well, he just needed all the help he could get.'

Wedding arrangements

Accidents

'Well, it's certainly been an eventful day already, and full marks to all the organizers for keeping us on our toes. The flat battery in the bride's limo was an original start – or non-start – and the "£5 OFF" stickers clearly visible on the groom's heels made for a real talking point. The vicar's uncontrollable hayfever was a truly inspired touch, topped off by the father of the groom taking two-and-a-half hours to drive the three miles from the ceremony to the reception. All in all, it's been a day that no one will forget in a hurry, and it's these funny little moments that we will all remember with a smile when we look back on this special day. At least that's what I keep telling the bride and groom. Now [feel frantically in all pockets]: where's my speech?'

Morning dress

'It's been great – if highly unusual – to see the best man and all the ushers dressed up in morning suits today. And if any of the bridesmaids are available and chocoholics, just think of the old advertising slogan, "P-p-p-p-pick up a penguin."'

Preparations

'I'm not saying they've overdone the preparations for this party, but last night I was asked to prepare a toast for the stand-in bride and groom.'

Priests

'There were so many priests at the altar today that I thought we were filming the new sequel to *Men in Black...*'

Stag do

'I'd love to tell you how, on his stag night, Steve got a tattoo on his behind, flirted with a seven-foot transvestite, had a brush with the police and woke up on a fishing boat off the coast of Norway. But as usual, he had three pints of light ale and crashed out in the corner.'

Tears

'Wow, what an emotional service! I know they say that it's good to shed a tear at a wedding, but I've never seen domino-crying on that scale before. Once someone in the first row had gone, the weeping epidemic spread right through the crowd and soon the whole room was awash. Even the organist was splashing great big tears onto her keyboard. I haven't seen anything like that since the great floods of 1992!'

Transport and travel

'The other day Harry rang me in a real panic. "How are we going to get to the wedding?" he said. "I'll give you a lift," I replied. "Why, what's the matter?" "Well, apparently Trish has got her own train," he said.'

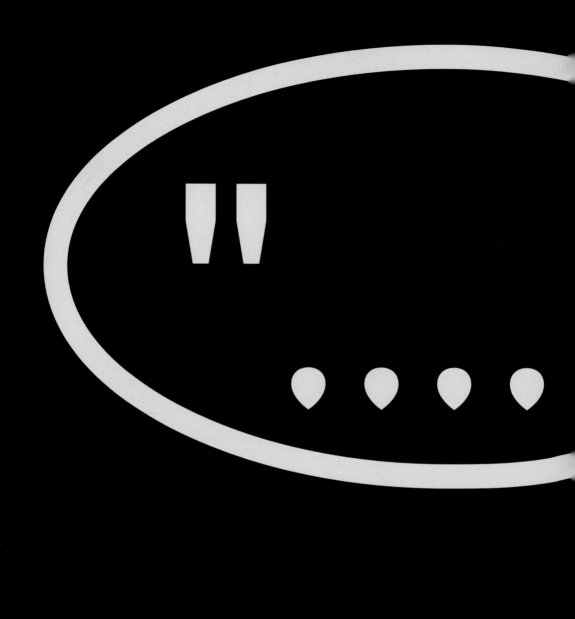

Great
sample
speeches

Inspiration for your speech

To inspire you to create a winning format for your speech, we've put together a selection of full-length sample speeches for you to choose from. Each one has a distinctive format that you can easily adapt to mould your unique material into a cohesive shape. No matter how well you research your anecdotes, and no matter how funny your stories and jokes, giving your material a recognizable framework will increase the impact of your material enormously. By simply replacing the anecdotes and characters in our sample speeches with your own material, you will quickly see how well each format could work for you. Sometimes a groom, unable to decide between two friends he's very close to, may opt to have them both as best men. But no matter how good they are, two best man speeches, one after the other, can begin to drag. So we've included a sample speech for a wedding in which two best men speak together (see pages 115–117). This is still relatively unusual and can make for a memorable speech with a difference.

Sample speech I

Sticking with tradition

'Ladies and gentlemen, Jean and Charles [bride's parents], Rodney and Rowena [groom's parents], Mr and Mrs Tate [the newlyweds, pause for a cheer here]...

'It is with great pleasure that I respond to Julian's [the groom's] kind toast on behalf of the bridesmaids. Even though he is too vain to be wearing his bottle-bottom National Health glasses today, I can confirm, Julian, that the bridesmaids do look as lovely as you just said, even though you were raising your glass to the waitress at the time.

'My other duty today is to regale you with stories of Julian's wicked past. I have to admit this has been tough to prepare for: not due to any shortage of stories but because most of them are too – how can I put this? – colourful to be retold in such refined company. Not counting you, Dave, of course [to one of the ushers].

'So in the end I thought: where better to begin than on that other auspicious date, thirty-odd (and his life has been odd) years ago, when Julian was born? In 1969, the year of Julian's birth, Neil Armstrong took his first tentative steps on the moon, as Julian took his own first baby steps. His mother tells me Julian also made his own "giant leap for mankind" but, unfortunately, Julian's was off the big slide in the park and resulted in a lovely little scar that I'm sure Helen will be seeing later...

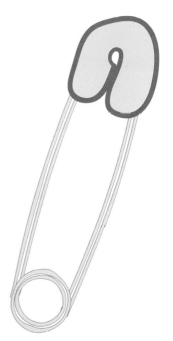

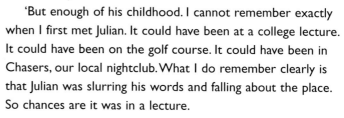

'Also in the year of his birth, the 50p piece was introduced into British currency, as Julian was making his own first little "pees"! It was also the year Sesame Street first hit our TV screens, and I'm told that Big Bird was a huge favourite of Julian's. That same year saw the publication of the first issue of Penthouse magazine and, er... I'm told that big birds have also been a huge favourite of Julian's.

'But enough of his childhood. I cannot remember exactly when I first met Julian. It could have been at a college lecture. It could have been on the golf course. It could have been in Chasers, our local nightclub. What I do remember clearly is that Julian was slurring his words and falling about the place. So chances are it was in a lecture.

'Julian is a fantastically generous and loyal friend. He's more than happy to come and collect you from your house and drive you to the golf course for a round at any time. He is also happy to coach you in your game with "encouraging" remarks at the very moment you are about to tee off.

'Julian is also a very trusting person. I remember one day when we went en masse to Leeds to visit an old mate for a party. Julian got lost on the way back from the pub and couldn't find where we were staying. Luckily, as he stumbled about the city centre, he bumped into a charming gang of lads who claimed they knew where he was staying and offered to escort him there.

'Arriving back at the student flat, Julian was so overwhelmed by how kind the locals had been, he offered to make them breakfast. A full English and several cups of tea later they left and Julian woke up his hungover mates to say how taken he'd been with his new friends. Taken, it later emerged, was indeed the word for it... his wallet, car keys, watch and mobile phone!

'Still, with Helen to look after him, Julian should be able to avoid such crises in future. I speak on behalf of all his mates, and with total sincerity, when I say that we still can't believe that anyone that lovely has agreed to take him on.

'Perhaps Helen should take some advice from that other paragon of great loveliness, Joanne Woodward, who has said of her own long marriage to Hollywood sex symbol Paul Newman: "Sexiness wears thin after a while and beauty fades, but to be married to a man who makes you laugh every day, ah, now that's a real treat." Helen, as you can see, he's no Paul Newman. But, just looking at him (or his scar), I think we can be sure that he will give you a laugh every day.

'And so ladies and gentlemen, I ask you to raise your glasses to a long, laughter-filled life together for the lovely couple – to Helen and Julian!'

Sample speech 2

The appraisal

'Ladies and gentlemen, it really is an honour to be standing in front of you today as best man to someone as special as Gary [the groom]. I must say that when he asked me, I was totally taken aback. But now I'm standing here I feel nothing but pride. Thanks for such an honour, mate.

'Okay, that was the nice, sincere part of the speech. Now it's time to get down to the nitty-gritty of embarrassing the very man who showed such faith, and yet such poor judgment, in choosing me.

'I thought long and hard about how to theme this speech, and then it suddenly dawned on me that I could use the skills I've picked up as a manager at work. I thought I'd write Katy [the bride] an appraisal of Gary.

'So, first things first: punctuality. Well, Katy, you must have known Gary long enough by now to know that he is not the world's greatest timekeeper. In fact, he's not the world's best when it comes to dates either. Only last week he told me how much he was looking forward to the wedding – on 7 July! Luckily I corrected him and here we are on the 8th... just! We were running late for most of the stag do, too, when Gary managed to miss the train to his own party. So Katy, you have been warned.

'Next we move on to: management skills. As we all know, one of the prerequisites of being a good manager is the art of diplomacy. And I think it's fair to say that Gary is not a man overly blessed with skills in this particular area. I remember we were sitting in French class when we were about 15 and we had a new teacher, Miss Simpson. She had just introduced herself and we were asking her some questions before class began when Gary piped up and asked her when her baby was due. Of course, there was no baby. Poor old, plump Miss Simpson went bright red and the rest of the class fell about. You did rather poorly in your 'O' level French, as I recall, Gary...

'Next on the agenda, Katy, has to be: career prospects. Now Gary is, as I'm sure we'll all agree, very competent at his job. In fact, he has moved steadily through the ranks and is doing very nicely, thanks. But I must say that things could have been so different. I'm told that during his student days, his part-time career at a large drinks company [alter as appropriate] was marred by his performance at the first Christmas party he attended all those years ago. Let's look at the ingredients of the disaster, shall we? There was Mr Hobbs [the groom], women and there was a free bar. Needless to say, Mr Hobbs helped himself to the bar, got rather drunk and rather loud and managed to finish the evening off by falling asleep on a desk, with his trousers neatly folded on the back of the chair. Sadly, it wasn't his desk – or chair – but his boss's. Oh, dear...

'Now what about: teamwork? Gary has always been a great team player. He's run the line for pretty much every football team he's tried to play in. He's washed the kit for several rugby clubs he's tried to join, and he makes a cracking tea when the lads play Sunday afternoon cricket. But seriously, though, Gary thrives in a team environment. He's unselfish and supportive when things are going badly, and that's what makes him such a great bloke. He can't play sport for toffee, mind you, but he's a great mascot...

'And finally, Katy, we move on to: extra-curricular activities. There's no point in denying that Gary thought of himself as a bit of a ladies' man at college. It turned out, however, that he was only chatting up different girls all the time because he couldn't find one that was interested. His favourite chat-up line at the time was: "We don't need to take our clothes off to have a good time. Let's just drink some cherry wine." I rest my case.

'So, Katy, that's my appraisal of Gary. It's too late to back out now. You'll just have to make a fist of it and see what happens. But what I do know is that he loves you very much and that you're going to have a great life together. To the happy couple!'

Sample speech 3
The political agenda

'Given the fact that Tim [the groom] is such an incredibly popular and successful man, it seems doubly amazing to me that he's asked me to be his best man. There must have been dozens of candidates. But then I am his oldest friend. I suppose the first thing I should do is to say thank you. And I suppose the second thing I should do is say sorry. Because while it is an honour to be standing here as your best man, it is also my duty to be really nasty about you, too.

'In fact, the first thing I did when I was asked to make this speech was ask Tim's doctor, who shall remain nameless, what he thought of the groom-to-be. The doctor said that, in his professional opinion, Tim was "clinically lazy, a compulsive liar and mildly neurotic". Shocked, I then asked for a second opinion. He replied: "Okay then, he's an ugly bugger with smelly feet."

'But enough of that. Let's get on with the speech. I thought, seeing as Tim has shown such an active and ideologically fluid interest in politics over the years, that it would be interesting to imagine what his election manifesto would look like, should he ever run for office. Now I know you should never discuss politics, sex or religion at the dinner table. But seeing as my only alternative is to tell the story about George W. Bush, a one-legged lady-of-the-night and the Reverend Ian Paisley, I think I'm on safer ground with the manifesto.

'Let us turn to education. Tim believes that every person should get the most out of the system. This explains why he spent two years in the third form at school, resat his A' levels twice and started two degrees before gaining a Second in Social Anthropology from Hull University. It has also been brought to my attention that, while at primary school, Tim availed himself of all the activities on offer, including taking part in the school Nativity play. He had a starring role as Third Sheep. Of course, right on cue his fellow sheep went "baa" and he went [pause] "moo".

'How about law and order? Tim has seen the activities of the police force up close, and is no stranger to the workings of the magistrates courts. After a rather merry evening at his local about a year ago, Tim decided to water the plants in someone's garden on the way home. Unfortunately, just as he was sprinkling the geraniums, two of Her Majesty's Constabulary happened upon him and he wound up in the nick for the night.

'Where does Tim stand on economics? Well, he most certainly believes in the free market. He's always coming up with hair-brained, get-rich-quick-schemes. A bit like the time he decided to hold a jumble sale in his front garden without telling his mum and dad. To make things worse, he wasn't just selling his old toys but also the contents of the family's front room. I must say that the brand-new video I picked up for 50p was the best bargain I've ever had. Lovejoy would have been proud!!

'What about foreign affairs? Well, Tim is all in favour. I've accompanied him on several trips abroad, all of which have involved attempted diplomatic "liaisons" with various local girls. But none was ever that successful. In fact, there was one time in France when he tried to use a romantic chat-up line. He meant to say to a rather stunning young mademoiselle: "Vous êtes très belle, je voudrais vous embrasser," meaning, "You're very beautiful, I'd like to kiss you." But instead he said: "Vous êtes très folle, je devrais vous enlacer", meaning: "You're very mad, I'm going to have to tie you up." Tim with his own version of the entente cordiale there...

'So there you have it: Tim's manifesto. As you can tell, he's a man of strong principles and fine ethics. So long as they disregard his politics, I know that he and Hayley will make a fantastic couple.

'Let me end now on a serious and sincere note by wishing today's lucky couple all the happiness in the world. Please join me in raising your glasses and be upstanding for the bride and groom!'

Sample speech 4

A day in the life of...

'Without a shadow of a doubt, this is the most nerve-wracking thing I have ever done. But at the same time it is a great honour to have been picked by Ken [the groom] as his best man. When he phoned to let me know, I nearly choked with surprise and I had a huge lump in my throat. That'll teach me to talk on the phone when I'm eating a kebab.

'Anyway, I thought long and hard about what I wanted to say in this speech. Obviously, Karen [the bride] has known Ken for many years. She's seen his career flourish, his hair fall out and his paunch widen.

'However, I realized that it's my duty to let Karen know what Ken was like BEFORE she met him. Obviously, since he met his beloved wife-to-be, Ken has been on his best behaviour. But I can assure you that hasn't always been the case.

'Ken and I have been best friends since primary school, so I have been witness to some of Ken's finer moments. I've also, of course, been witness to some of his less than fine moments. And, naturally, it's those moments that I feel I should tell Karen about – in front of just about everyone Ken cares about.

'How best to catalogue such a huge number of embarrassing moments? Well, I thought I would put them together on a CV to support Ken's application for the job of Karen's husband. OK, so he's already landed the job – but just bear with me...

'Let's start with his qualifications, shall we? An impressive ten O' levels, three A' levels and a second class honours degree in Sports Science from Lancaster University. Ken also holds various gymnastics badges, 17 merit badges (including needlework!) from Scouts, and a Winner's Certificate – from our Club 18–30 holiday to Santa Ponsa, Majorca – in the Drink-As-Much-Sangria-As-You-Can-Before-Passing-Out contest, 1993.

'Let us take a look now in more detail at Ken's glittering academic career.

'1981–1983: Busy Bee nursery school. [mimicking the groom's voice] "I spent three years honing my excellent communication skills at this prestigious school, where my love of drama flourished. I appeared in several productions, playing Lead Toadstool, Second Sheep and Mr Frog, before a controversial starring role as Pontius Pilate in the school Nativity play."

'1983–1989: Clifton Manor primary school. "In a distinguished career at Clifton, I became one of the most popular boys in the school. This was because, for several years, I conned my mum into giving me dinner money, when in fact we were given lunch at the school. I used this money to build up a small stock of sweets, comics and pictures of Page 3 models, which formed the basis of a highly successful black market operation run from behind the athletics equipment hut.

'1989–1994: Stoneybrook secondary school. "As well as a successful record in both O' and A' levels at Stoneybrook, I was also the first student to dye my hair orange for mufti day, and the only student to receive a suspension for drinking cider in the language lab. In the sporting arena, I excelled in the area of cross-country, holding the school record for nearly two years. Unfortunately, the title was taken away from me in a rather ignominious fashion, when the games master realized that the time I had recorded was, in fact, close to the world record for 5,000 metres. I had, of course, hidden in a bush for the duration of the race, reappearing, complete with muddy legs and flushed cheeks, only a few minutes later to jog home. My appeal, lodged with the International Athletics Federation in 1992, is pending."

'1995–1999: Lancaster University. "While at college, I was an active member of the student body. I joined the Real Ale Society, the Wine Society and the Soul, Funk & Reggae Society, and was a regular attender at all the social events organized by each. I also gained several honours during my time there. I am still the only Sports Science student ever to be reprimanded for poor attendance in lectures, having only managed four in six terms. I held the Yard of Ale record for three terms and am still, to my knowledge, the only student to have run up a four-figure overdraft with three of the five major high street banks.

'19 March, 2000 (the day I met Karen) – present: "I am now enjoying the best time of my life, and continue to be the luckiest man alive since meeting the love of my life."

'Ladies and gentlemen, I give you the groom and his wonderful, beautiful bride.'

Sample speech 5
The Two Ronnies

This speech can be used when there are two best men; let's call them Best Man 1 (BM1) and Best Man 2 (**BM2**). Don't try and rehearse too much and make sure you read it from cards. Trying to learn it verbatim and perform without prompts seldom works as well.

BM1 'Good evening. Before we get on with the formal parts of the speech, Tim and I would just like to read out some headlines.'

BM2 [In a newsreader's voice] 'Good evening and here is the news... from Dave's [the groom] past...'

BM1 '19 February, 1975: A Peterborough couple gave birth today to their son David Algernon Smith, who weighed in at a rather skinny 6lb 11oz. The couple, Peter and Lorraine, were said to be delighted with the newest edition to their family, although Mr Smith was overheard as saying: "I thought you said it was going to be a girl, mother." 'When asked about the baby's diminutive size, Mrs Smith said: "I'm sure he'll put on weight quickly." How right Mrs Smith was then and has been ever since...'

BM2 '26 May, 1989: A young Peterborough boy, David Smith, was thrown out of the Scouts today, after an internal inquiry, led by Bagheera and Akela, found the rascal guilty of stealing a bottle of wine from a local fête. Smith was unavailable for comment, having been sent to his room without tea and a smack across the back of his legs. 'The boy's parents were said to be upset and dismayed, according to a close family source.'

BM1   '28 September, 1993: Liverpool University welcomed a highly acclaimed schoolboy academic through its doors, today. David Smith, fresh from his triumphant two Cs and a D at A' level, took his seat in the geography department. He is said to be eager to make the most of his opportunity and wants to be a model student in the tertiary education system.

'"This is a great chance for me to change the way geography is perceived around the world," said Smith on the steps of the Red Lion. "I'm sick of it being ridiculed as a dossers' subject, full of rejects and wannabe town planners," enthused the uncharacteristically frank youngster, known as Smudge by his small circle of friends and fellow layabouts. "I aim to give my degree my best shot and will settle for nothing less than a First."'

BM2 '7 July, 1994: David 'Smudge' Smith was un-cordially invited to "leave the university and never darken the geography department's door again" by leading town planning lecturer 'Pongo' Watson. Professor Watson cited several reasons for the dismissal of Smith, concluding that: "The main reason he has been asked to leave is because unlike most students – who usually have poor attendance records – Mr Smith has no attendance record at all."'
'When given the news in bed, at three o'clock this afternoon, a tight-lipped Smith stated: "I'm off to the Union to get pissed."'

BM1 '9 October 1996: Dave 'Hound Dog' Smith was spotted talking to a mystery blonde in Shakers nightclub this evening. Having downed several vodkas, three pints of cider and a quantity of Dubonnet, the normally reserved Smith is said to have tackled the stunner – later identified as Kerry Watson, 26, from Plaistow – as she danced with friends. He later claimed in court that he wasn't trying to 'tackle' her but had lost his footing while crossing the dance floor, stumbled and reached out for the nearest thing available – Ms Watson's chest. After a verbal exchange, the two were seen leaving together.'

BM2: 'And that was the news. So it's goodnight from me...'

BM1: 'And goodnight from him.'

Sample speech 6

Men in the movies

'Distinguished guests, ladies, gentlemen, boys and girls, I've been dreading introducing the final speaker today, as it's me!

'Nevertheless, it's an honour, nay a privilege, to be standing here today as Don's best man. Now's my chance to take just a few moments to reflect upon what is a wonderful and poignant day for Don and Gwen.

'As many of you already know, my friendship with Don is lifelong. Which presents me with my first challenge today: how to encapsulate in five minutes (I promise to be that short), the sum of our 30 years of friendship.

'How, I asked myself when I lay down upon my chaise-longue to pen this masterpiece, can I give you a flavour of our countless childhood adventures and quests, our loyalties and rivalries and, above all, our ongoing, mutual and fervent desire to play the hero, defeat the baddies, plunder the treasure and get the girl?

'Suddenly, I had an idea. What better way, I thought to myself reclining in my local opium den, than to use movies as

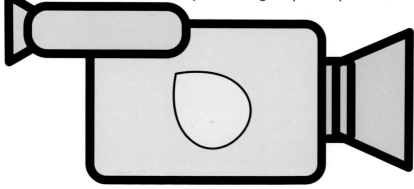

reference points to our past? So I've selected just a handful that will give you a candid view of Don – boy and man.

'The first film that comes to mind is the classic western *The Magnificent Seven*. We were so into the film as kids. We'd learn lines from the film and play our characters with as much realism as possible... sort of method acting for infants.

'I played Vin, Steve McQueen's brooding, silent hero – the sharp-shooting, good-looking one whom girls adore and bandits fear. I had the whole outfit – hat, gun holsters, the lot.

'Don was very jealous. He played Chris, Yul Brynner's character, the simmering, compassionate leader of the Seven. Hardly a ladies' man.

'One day at school just after the Christmas hols, Don disappeared just before break. I was about to start fending off "de feelthy greengos" alone, when through the playground gates he burst with an oh-so-improved, Yul Brynner outfit on!

'He was dressed head to toe in black – with brand-new, gun holsters, a pair of sparkling Colt 45s, and real leatherette cowboy boots. However, never one to overlook a detail, Don was also sporting a pink bathing cap, to give him that authentic bald look. What a pro! (Today, of course, he doesn't really need the cap...)

'Then there was another old favourite of ours, *The Hound of the Baskervilles*. Whenever we played Holmes and Watson, I was always the great detective: studious, erudite, heroic, brilliant. Don was always Dr Watson: fat, bumbling, clueless and comical. You begin to see a pattern emerging?

'However, the tables finally turned – or so Don thought – when we saw the trailer for *Star Wars*. Before we went to watch the movie, Don, marginally ahead of me in the puberty stakes, staked his claim to play Luke Skywalker, the central character – the Jedi who's forever "using the force" and battling "the dark side". I was relegated to being Han Solo.

'Unluckily for Don, Han Solo turned out to be way cooler and more rebellious than Luke. He had an oversize shaggy sidekick – as did I, I suppose – called Chewbacca (or Don, in my case). And crucially, Han bagged beautiful Princess Leia! From the moment we came out of that movie, a crestfallen Don never spoke of playing characters in films again.

'But no matter how old we were, there was always a movie that seemed to perfectly reflect our place in the world. Visiting Don at his college digs was like a scene from *Withnail and I*, with Don covering his body in Deep Heat to keep warm as he'd run out of coins for the electricity meter!

'And when he got his first job as a journalist, albeit as a sub-editor on *Tiddlywinks Monthly* – or whatever the title was – going for a drink with Don was like accompanying Orson Welles, the media mogul in *Citizen Kane*. Except Don could never buy a round, let alone a newspaper empire.

'But surely the greatest day in Don's life was when he met the beautiful, kind and inspiring Gwen – a scene reminiscent of when Viggo Mortensen and Liv Tyler hook up in *The Lord of the Rings*. In fact, the night it happened, soppy old Don said he thought Gwen must be from heaven... or even Rivendell!

'Congratulations Don, it's been a lifelong pleasure to play the hero to your sidekick, mate. Together we defeated our share of baddies and plundered the treasure. But today, I'm happy to say, it's you who's got the girl. And what a girl she is. Ladies and gentlemen, I give you the adorable couple – the bride and groom – Don and Gwen.'

Sample speech 7
The seven deadly sins

'When Alan asked me to be his best man, the sense of honour I felt was mixed up with a faint foreboding. How would he take it if I spilled the beans and told everyone the whole truth?

'Alan soon reassured me that he wanted a warts-and all speech, and Angela promised me she wouldn't hold it against me if she found out anything she'd rather not know. So, you've only got yourselves to blame if you're not on speaking terms on the honeymoon...

'When Alan met Angela, he told me he'd met a fabulous girl with apparently no faults at all. "She's an angel by name and an angel by nature," he said. Two years later he swears his opinion hasn't changed. So I hope Angela realizes that the guy she's chosen to spend her life with is a bit of a devil.

'They say that opposites attract – well, if Angela is a paragon of virtue, Alan certainly has a long career of vice behind him!

'Alan once told me that he never understood the expression "ugly as sin", because he had always found sin rather attractive. Well, as we all know, there are seven deadly sins. Perhaps it's just a coincidence that this was the number of pints Alan downed most nights.

'So let's take a close look at Alan's diabolical talent for sin...

'Let's start with avarice, since the Bible tells us that the love of money is the root of all evil. Now this may be my biggest

challenge, since all of Alan's drinking companions are more acquainted with his huge talent for spending money rather than for making it.

'However, let me remind you that when he arrived at college he was signed up to do business studies and apparently fancied himself as a future tycoon. This ambition only came a cropper because another of his vices stood in the way: sloth.

'Yes, Alan realized that in the business world you have to work hard to make your way, so he dropped business for French. As he has a French mum (to mum: Bonjour madame!) and is already virtually bilingual, this was not perhaps the most challenging of studies to pursue.

'I remember Alan begging me to tell him the plot of one of our set books on the way to the literature exam. He hadn't read it, but that didn't stop him getting a better grade than me. Luck of the Devil, I suppose.

'As for wrath, or anger, this was usually on display after 11pm, when the barman wouldn't serve him another drink. Alan is also notoriously belligerent on the football field. He once threatened to put the referee into hospital. Later that night, he was spotted in the pub with his arms around the offending official, telling him that he really loved him and could he borrow a tenner?

'Next up it's gluttony. This was shown not only in Alan's consumption of beer, but also by his prodigious appetite in the curry house after closing time.

'The Taj Mahal in the high street was the setting for Alan's greatest displays of envy too. Whatever he ordered, he always decided that he preferred our choice to his own, and if we had to go to the toilet we would often find our plates almost empty when we got back. He would never own up to it.

'That's his pride you see: one of the deadliest of the seven. Alan can never admit to his mistakes. Once he fell asleep on the train after a heavy night drinking and woke up in Brighton. He maintained afterwards that he had always wanted to sleep on the beach under the stars.

'Another example of Alan's envious side was the sarcastic reaction whenever any of his mates managed to get a steady girlfriend. He was never known to have one, and that brings me to the one you've all been waiting for: lust. For Alan, this was restricted to flicking through the underwear pages in his mum's mail-order catalogue.

'Anyway all that is history. Alan is a reformed character now that he has found his angel and is on the way to becoming a saint. So all that remains for me is to wish them all the best. May their life together be heaven on earth!

'Ladies and gentlemen, please raise your glasses in honour of Alan and Angela – our happy and virtuous couple!'

Sample speech 8
Desert island discs

This speech will work best if you are able to play snatches of the tunes you've chosen as you go along.

'Ladies and gentlemen, I am greatly honoured to have been given the job of best man for Tom. Ever since he asked me to make this speech, I have been trying to work out exactly how to hit that winning blend of comedy and sincerity, with a hint of humiliation. Then last night I decided to stop trying so hard, forget the balance and go for all-out humiliation.

'Seriously though, for those of us who know Tom well, one of his defining characteristics is the fact that he's something of a Radio 4 bore, so to help give you an idea of his true personality I've chosen the theme of one of his favourite shows – *Desert Island Discs*. Of course the twist here is that I get to choose the records that best sum him up, though I have included a few of his own favourites as well.

'So, where to start? Well, my castaway this week is a balding 32-year-old ex-hippie who thinks novelty ties are cool, has three points on his driving licence (for driving too slowly) and enjoys a late-night snack of a tuna and chocolate spread sandwich. And so to our first record...

'Those of us who have had the privilege of accompanying Tom on his journey through the British education system will be aware of his love of discussion and heated political debate. Having racked my brains for the best song to illustrate the sophisticated level of Tom's debate, I came up with one of Tom's personal favourites. (Play tune). That's right, it's Cliff Richard's *Mistletoe and Wine* – not only dealing with the deeper issues in life but also, to quote Tom, has "a rousing melody and Is, simply, a classic". What more is there to say?

'Next record. Now we all know of Tom's refined culinary tastes and love of gourmet food. At first I thought I'd show this with that seminal hit, *Two Pints of Lager and a Packet of Crisps Please*. Then I thought about the Pizza Hut jingle. But then I remembered the aftermath of all the numerous eating-and-drinking sessions I've enjoyed with Tom over the years and the choice was obvious: (play Johnny Cash's *Ring of Fire*). Enough said. Let's move on.

'One of the most touching of Tom's endearing attributes is his combination of confidence and utter incompetence, that is, the things he's proudest of tend to be the things he's worst at. Take dancing. If you were to ask Tom, I'm sure he would tell you that he is a whirling diva on the dance floor. Well, I think the time has come to let you down gently, Tom. A quick poll of your nearest and dearest – and an examination of the injuries of many innocent bystanders – suggests you may not be the John Travolta you think you are. (Play tune.) Yep, *Disco Duck* by Rick Dees and his Cast of Idiots is the song that best reflects your dancing talents...

'Staying with the dancing theme, Tom came to me a few weeks ago to say that his new bride Linda had given him the task of choosing tonight's first dance. Linda, I don't know what possessed you, but I think I deserve the credit for saving you from having to start your married life with a strut to Billy Ray Cyrus's *Achy Breaky Heart*. Or this (play Daniel Beddingfield's *Gotta Get Through This*), Tom's other idea. Happily the job was reassigned before any damage was done.

(Play *Y Viva Espana*) 'With music being such an important part of Tom's life it was inevitable that his favourite songs would influence the major decisions in his life. Ever since he was a small boy *Y Viva Espana* has been a firm favourite. In line with Tom's sophisticated tastes and love of the exotic, I believe the couple plan to honeymoon in an exclusive location, somewhere between Fuengirola and Torremolinos. From what I can gather he's even booked an awning...

'On Tom's wedding day, it's only right that I spend a little time on his quest to find the perfect girl. His success with women is legendary and on this one I was spoilt for choice. A large section of his record collection is made up of songs women have sent him to try and convey their feelings, such as this: (play *You're So Vain*). Or this: (play *Tainted Love*).

'Finally ladies and gentlemen, Tom is my oldest and closest friend and I am proud to have been able to torment him in this way. The last choice tonight is mine and I would like to dedicate Phil Collins' *Groovy Kind of Love* to the happy couple and wish them love and laughter now and always. (Play *Groovy Kind of Love*)

'Please be upstanding and raise a glass to Tom and Linda.'

Sample speech 9
Love lyrics

'Ladies and gentlemen, when I was asked to give a best man's speech I decided that I wouldn't be doing my duty unless I gave everyone an insight into the life and character of my best friend, Martin.

'But where was I to start? I could have spoken about Martin's love of cars, but since he has written off three of them in five years, it's probably better to avoid that subject. Or I could have mentioned his taste in clothing, but since his favourite garment is a T-shirt that says "Dip me in chocolate and feed me to the bears", I figured it might be a good idea to gloss over that part of his life too.

'What some of you might not realize is that Martin loves song lyrics. If there's a karaoke machine at a local pub, nothing can stop him from getting on the stage and belting out the lyrics of *My Way*.

'Songs have played an important role in his life. He was the only boy at our school who cried when Take That split up. For days afterwards he could be seen sobbing and gently singing *Relight My Fire*. And he could do all the hand movements: he was a bit of a sorry lad.

'(I recently discovered that he tried to get an audition for Pop Idol, which just goes to show that older doesn't necessarily mean wiser.)

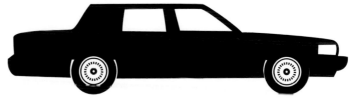

'Nevertheless, as he grew older, his tastes became more mature. Slightly. He is the only sales manager I have ever met who knows the words to all of Westlife's songs, for instance.

'Samantha tells me that Martin was an old-fashioned lover. He would sit outside her house and sing to her. He only asked her to marry her when she told him that she loved Kylie Minogue as much as he did.

'But Martin, I've got something to tell you. Sam was only saying that to please you. She can't stand Kylie Minogue. She thinks that *I Should Be so Lucky* is cheesy. She reckons *Can't Get You Out Of My Head* is the most overrated song of all time. And as soon as you get back from honeymoon, she's going to accidentally throw out your prized *Soap Stars Sing the Classics* album and buy you some decent music.

'Actually, it's not true. Martin and Samantha share their taste for the good things in life; fine wines, good food and even, dare I say it, Westlife.

'So, if I had to think of the words of a song that sums up their life together, I'd pick the following – *You Can't Hurry Love*. It's a wonderful Motown classic and, because Martin and Samantha have been together for six years, it seems very appropriate.

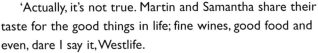

'And how about a song to sum up how they feel now? For Samantha to sing to Martin, I don't think you could do better than *You're The One That I Want* from the soundtrack of Grease. And for Martin to sing for Sam, I think it would have to be Eric Clapton's *You Look Wonderful Tonight.*

'Oh, and there's one more song that I think they could both truthfully sing to each other. It's a song that was first recorded by Gladys Knight: *You're the Best Thing That Ever Happened To Me.*

'As I'm sure you'd all agree, Sam and Martin go wonderfully together. I know there will always be lots of exciting tracks on their CD player. And I hope that whatever songs they sing, there will always be harmony between them.

'They're a fantastic couple and I know we all wish them the very best. Can you please raise your glasses in a toast to Samantha and Martin.'

Sample speech 10
Literary inspiration

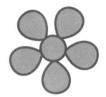

'Distinguished guests, ladies and gentlemen, girls and boys. I am very happy to be here today as James' best man and to have this chance to thank you all on behalf of the bridesmaids.

'I'm sure you'd all agree that the scene in front of us today could have come from a film, a play or a book. And this is hardly a coincidence, because James, as some of you will know, is a pretty bookish sort of a fellow. In fact, we first met in Blackwell's bookshop in Oxford. He was looking at the books in the philosophy section and I was cleaning the floor.

'Now you might think that James is a pretty laid-back sort of guy, but I'm getting the impression he's actually been quite wound up about the forthcoming nuptials. For example, last week, as we were having a drink and chatting about the great day, James let slip that he has made a list of his top ten books of all time. When I saw it, I was struck by how appropriate they were for what James has in store for him.

'Number ten was *War and Peace* and number nine was *Crime and Punishment*. So quite a strong Russian theme there. *Catch 22* was in there too, I remember. That's the one where the main character pretends to be mad in order to avoid going to war, but the doctor says that you have to be sane to want to avoid going to war. Nuff said.

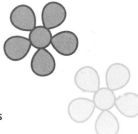

'Number seven was Nick Hornby's *How To Be Good*. This one may be a veiled reference to James' stag night, but my mind's gone blank and I simply can't quite remember.

'Straight in at number six is *The Curious Incident of the Dog in the Night-time*. I'll just pause for a moment's silence here while you all add in your own punchline...

'Number five was *Great Expectations*. I don't think Emily will have many of those. *Hard Times* would be a better choice.

'Number four was *Atonement* – well, James will be doing plenty of that if the truth about the stag night ever emerges.

'Number three baffled me for a long time – it was volume seven of the *Encyclopaedia Britannica*. Until I looked on the spine, where it said "How to Hug".

'Sorry about that.

'Number two was Homer's *Odyssey*. Well, fair enough. After all, marriage is a long journey in sometimes choppy seas, a stirring adventure with happiness awaiting you at the end. And there's a one-eyed monster involved too.

'Finally, number one was a very strange choice indeed – it was *Schott's Miscellany*.

'Hardly a book that would help you much with the intricacies of modern marriage, I thought. I hunted down a copy in Blackwell's (after I'd finished emptying the bins and taking out the rubbish) and had a browse. Of course, as you do, I found some useful stuff. How to tie a sari, for example, or commonly misspelled words like "diarrhoea" or "broccoli" – but nothing much about marriage.

'But then I began to see a theme. There's a page of hangover cures. (From the extensive research I did, I would recommend the one called "The Lazenby"). There's a page of palindromes – that's words and phrases that spell the same backwards as forwards to you and me – and I found this: "Are we not drawn onward, we few, drawn onward to new era?" What could be more suitable for a marriage?

'Or how about this quote from A P Herbert: "The critical period in matrimony is breakfast time." Just remember that, James. No farting over the cornflakes.

'Or how about the fact that you burn off between six and 11 calories per minute during sex? Though in James' case... Sorry.

'So you see it may be that *Schott's Miscellany* holds the key to marital happiness. But actually the book that I would say was the most appropriate for today was one that would always appear on my top ten list – *Lucky Jim*!

'And on that note, let me propose a toast to today's lovely, happy couple. Ladies and gentlemen, please raise your glasses: to the bride and groom!'

Sample speech 11
The gadget freak

'Ladies and Gentlemen, as Neville's best man and one of his oldest friends, it's my job this evening to give you an insight into what he's really like, and what Kayleigh, for better of for worse, has taken on...

'When I started to think about what I could say today, it struck me the one thing that everyone knows about Neville, is his fascination – some would say his obsession – with gadgets.

'Anyone who has seen the look of glee in his eyes when he spots the Innovations catalogue dropping out of the Sunday paper knows what I'm talking about. Neville is a man who would rather consult his digital weather forecaster than look out of the window to see if it's raining.

'To paraphrase Joseph Conrad, "You shall judge a man by his gadgets as well as by his friends." So I think it would be interesting to take a look at Neville's favourite gizmos and see what they say about the man.

'First up, the satellite navigation system he has in his car, which he uses on every journey he makes – even to drive the quarter of a mile to the newsagent's. This tells us that Neville is a lazy sod with an underdeveloped sense of direction, certainly, but it also tells us something more fundamental. Most of us here will have seen another of Nev's gadgets – his amazing watch. In case Nev hasn't yet gone through its features with you – and if he hasn't, you can count yourself one of the lucky few – it can show you your altitude, whether it's going to rain, what direction you're facing, and it probably has a built-in breathalyser as well.

'In fact the only thing it doesn't do is actually tell the time.

'Which is very appropriate, as Neville has never shown the slightest sign of understanding what the concept of time is. One thing you can depend on is that Neville will always be late. In the language of gadgets, "late" is his default setting.

'One time when a bunch of us went to Scotland for a golfing weekend he missed the plane going out, he turned up that evening but missed our teeing off time the next morning, and then although he came with us to the airport he managed to miss the plane coming back too. Although that might have been something to do with the fact that he drank rather a lot the night before and was in the airport bogs throwing up when our flight was called. Nice one Nev.

'What about Nev's famous Freeview box? He bought it about two years ago despite knowing that you can't get Freeview where he lives because of all the high buildings.

'Perhaps this reflects Nev's character. A constant search for new opportunities – even if it's only the opportunity to watch more TV. A sense of optimism – that the box will work even when the man in Currys says that it won't – a refusal to take no for an answer, even a desire to push the boundaries of technology... Personally I suspect it reflects nothing more than good old-fashioned stupidity, but you never know.

'Nev's reliance on his sat nav shows a man who has never had any plan in life – a free spirit who simply wanders from opportunity to opportunity. In fact, it's true to say that Neville doesn't have the faintest idea what he wants to do when he grows up. If that is, he ever grows up.

'But before I finish I would like to talk about Nev's penknife. It's got about 50 or so blades, saws, screwdrivers and tweezers. It even has one of those handy tools for getting stones out of horses' hooves.

'Why is this significant? Because, although it pains me as best man to say anything nice about Neville at his wedding, it shows that Kayleigh is not completely mad to be marrying this man.

'Because, Kayleigh, your new husband may not have any plan to ensure he has enough money to support you, and although he will probably drive you mad with his poor timekeeping, the fact that he carries a tool for getting stones out of horses' hooves despite knowing nothing about horses, and even less about stones, is a good sign of something we all know...

'Neville is one of those rare people who is always ready to help a friend, a stranger, or even a horse, in their time of need. And that, in my book, marks him out as a true friend and an all-round great bloke – one that (almost) deserves a lovely person like you, Kayleigh, to be his beautiful bride. And one it has been an absolute privilege to be best man for.

'So I'd like to ask you all to join me in wishing them both a very happy life together, with a toast to the bride and groom...'

Sample speech 12
The telly addict

'Good evening everyone. For those of you who don't know me, I'm Colin, Bryan's best man, and Bryan's been my friend since way back when we were at primary school together in Solihull.

'The sad truth about Bryan is that he has to get three or four in every night. Telly programmes that is. In fact, it wouldn't be an exaggeration to say that he is a bit of a telly addict. I've seen him sit on the sofa, barely moving for hours on end, on beautiful summer days when everyone else is outside getting a tan.

'Now they say that watching TV is a waste of time, but I think you can probably get quite a lot from it – especially if you have Bryan's extreme viewing habits.

'So the question I'd like to ask tonight is this: how much of the Bryan we have come to know and love is attributable to his telly watching?

'I think it's fair to say that Bryan has, without a doubt, the world's worst taste in music. If you don't believe me have a flick through his CD collection. The Dooleys! Kenny Loggins! The Carpenters! A bigger collection of absolute rubbish is impossible to imagine. How can anyone like this stuff?

'Well, ladies and gentlemen, I believe I know the answer to this question. As eight-year-olds we used to scuttle home from school together so that we could watch *Blue Peter*.

'I used to love learning how to make cool things and seeing John Noakes bravely leaping out of planes or climbing chimney stacks. But for Bryan the highlight was the *Blue Peter* theme tune, an annoying sea shanty to which he used to do a little dance.

'No Bryan, I haven't forgotten that. It's my theory that Bryan's taste in music is a result of being exposed to this sea shanty in his formative years. And here's his dance again folks! (Look at groom expectantly). No? Perhaps later on the dance floor then.

'Bryan is also someone who likes the sound of his own voice. I'll grudgingly admit that he can tell a good joke, but give him a pint or two and he'll start one of his shaggy dog stories and frequently end up not remembering the punch line – if there ever was one.

'Where did he get this penchant for story telling? Well, I can't prove anything, but I do remember that at the end of Blue Peter I would usually get up and go outside to play football, leaving Bryan to watch ... *Jackanory*. Mmmmm.

'What else do we know about Bryan? He is a free spirit – a truly strong person. He is capable of following a chosen course of action with steely determination despite levels of ridicule that would have surely discouraged normal people.

'Just the qualities, in fact, that one learns from a near psychopathic devotion to watching *Coronation Street*.

'I worked out the other day that he has spent more time watching Corry than... he has been alive. Well that's probably because I am rubbish at maths. Unlike Bryan here, who, thanks to his devotion to *Countdown* (due to a partiality to Carol Vorderman's bum, he once confided to me) has an amazing way with numbers.

'Another of Bryan's lifelong obsessions is the past. He always watches historical documentaries, films like *Elizabeth* and *Troy*, and he never misses an episode of *Time Team*. The rumours that Tracy actually unearthed Bryan at an architectural dig have yet to be confirmed.

'What we do know – and celebrate – today is that Bryan did at last manage to get off his behind and go out and meet someone very special. Tracy, it's a tribute to your sunny personality, sublime sense of humour and seductive wiles that you managed to tear our Bry away from the little box and get him to go out and get a life.

'Yes, it's thanks to Tracy that Bryan is the man that he is today – not indoors watching nonsense but here with his family and friends, celebrating his marriage to the beautiful, graceful and charming Tracy.

'Tracy, thanks to you we've all come to know a bit more about the great guy you're marrying today. I can assure you that with Bryan in your life you will never be bored. Except perhaps by his shaggy dog stories.

'Oh and by the way: Bryan says could you all leave by ten sharp tonight because *Desperate Housewives* is on? Thanks.

'So ladies and gentlemen, please join me in a toast to Bryan and Tracy.'

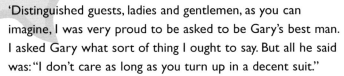

Sample speech 13

Written in the stars

'Distinguished guests, ladies and gentlemen, as you can imagine, I was very proud to be asked to be Gary's best man. I asked Gary what sort of thing I ought to say. But all he said was: "I don't care as long as you turn up in a decent suit."

'So I thought I'd talk about one of Gary's passions. And I don't mean Judy. As many of you will know, Gary has always been very keen on horoscopes. He believes that you can read the future in the stars. Which is quite unusual for an Aquarius, actually...

'Even when we were back at school, I can vividly remember us lying on his parents' lawn one night and staring up into the night sky. And he said to me: "Look at all those little twinkling points of light. It must mean something." This was an early indication of his interest in astrology. Either that, or a sign that we'd drunk too much cider.

'As we grew older, the stars continued to play an important part in Gary's life. At local discos, he would go up to girls, give them a wink, and say: "You must be Pisces. I think we could be compatible." He would then spend the rest of the evening wondering why none of them wanted anything to do with him.

'At such times there was indeed something of the fish about him.

'However, as you all know, he eventually did meet Judy, they got together and his chat up lines improved to the extent that she agreed to marry him.

'What, then, do the stars hold in store for today's happy couple? I nipped down to the library to see if I could give them any useful astrological guidance...

'Gary, as I say, is an Aquarius – an air sign. Hot air usually, in Gary's case. Aquarians are known to be eccentric, independent and unpredictable. Which is about as kind a summary of Gary's legendary dress sense as anyone could offer.

'According to the horoscopes Aquarians are very quick to adopt labour-saving devices. Anyone who saw Gary watching the World Cup with a can of beer in one hand and the TV remote control in the other will know just how accurate this is.

'I had a look to see if there are any famous Aquarians. One I came up with was the Indian politician, Gandhi. But as he lived on a diet of lentils and spent hours meditating to remove lustful thoughts, I'm not sure he'd be a great example to the young married couple.

'Other famous Aquarians include Germaine Greer, Abraham Lincoln, Oprah Winfrey and Bob Marley.

'Gary certainly shares many qualities with this illustrious bunch. He has Bob Marley's sense of urgency, Oprah's dietary discipline, and Germaine Greer's argumentative nature (just not her brains, unfortunately). But unlike Abe Lincoln, Gary isn't exactly a culture vulture: he wouldn't be seen dead in a theatre, for instance.

'Now Judy is a Leo – a fire sign. I looked it up and found out that Leos have a fine sense of drama and they adore pageantry. Which doubtless explains the wonderful "wedding show" that we're enjoying today, from the menu to the flowers to the table decorations.

'And I looked up famous Leos too. These include Napoleon and President Clinton. So Gary should be all right, as long as he can put up with a wife who's power mad and sex crazed. Somehow, I think he'll manage.

'To be serious for a moment, Aquarians are dependable, steady, sensible and kind. And they want to make the world a better place. And I think that describes Gary well.

'On the other hand, Leos are determined, astonishingly loyal, loving and generous. And that just about sums up Judy.

'Evidently, when these two star signs get together, there are sparks, passion and lots of fun. Everyone who has had the pleasure to know Gary and Judy can see that their relationship will be eventful, lively and loving.

'So let's forget the horoscopes: as far as we're all concerned, Gary and Judy are the real stars. Can you please be upstanding and raise your glasses as we toast – the bride and groom!'

Sample speech 14
Language barrier

'Distinguished guests, ladies and gentlemen, boys and girls. I am very happy to be here today as Tim's best man, and also to have this chance to thank you all on behalf of the bridesmaids.

'I am not quite sure why Tim chose me to be his best man. After all, Tim and I have known each other for a very long time – too long, some of you may say – and there are many secrets that I could reveal, unless a large quantity of used notes appears very quickly...

'But no, that would be all too easy. I am very honoured to be chosen, and Tim, your secrets are safe with me – at least while I'm sober.

'Now as most of you will know, Sonia is from Israel, and she and Tim met when she was studying English in Manchester. Of course, she and Tim speak completely different languages, so in that respect they are just like any other married couple.

'As Tim was very happy, proud and pleased to be dating a girl as gorgeous as Sonia, he introduced me to her early on in their relationship. And I think it would be fair to say that, since Tim didn't know any Hebrew, communication between them at that stage was more physical than verbal.

'Let me rephrase. Let us just say that mimes and silly gestures have never been so tender... especially the one where Tim was pretending to be a teapot.

'As time went by, as with any couple, the rapport between them developed to such a point that Sonia barely needed to say anything at all before Tim would hurry to do what she said. And if my wife is listening...

'In fact, I've always thought that the relationship between Tim and Sonia was based on a sense of equality. They were equals In the sense that Sonia couldn't always express what she wanted because she spoke another language, and Tim couldn't express what he wanted... because he was a man.

'Of course, in this spirit of give and take, Tim felt he should try to learn a little Hebrew at the same time. Tim was a bit of a cheapskate in those days, and I remember that he acquired a very old Hebrew phrasebook from a second-hand bookshop for just a few pence so that he could learn some useful phrases for when he and Sonia were dating.

The old Boy Scouts' advice to "be prepared" was one that Tim followed rigorously.

'I remember one day coming across the phrasebook on the kitchen table in the house we shared in Headington, and Tim had highlighted some phrases – presumably the ones he was expecting to use.

'Some of these phrases were what you'd expect, if a little out-of-date. Things like – (read from actual phrasebook) – and you'll have to excuse my pronunciation at this point: "ani meqabel beratzon et hazmanatkha", which means "I willingly accept your invitation". And "hayesh birtzonkha lesaheq mishaq ehad beshah", meaning, "May I invite you to waltz?"

'But others were a bit puzzling. I remember seeing that he had highlighted "heykhan efshar lirhotz", which apparently means: "Where can I wash my hands?" And "ani mehapes roves-tzayid": "I am looking for a shotgun".

'Phrasebooks never quite give you the information you need, do they? Would Tim ever need a phrase from page 113: "Please show me rubber toys"? Or the gem on page 64: "Would you like me to do the washing-up?" I don't know about you, but I can't imagine Tim ever needing this last one.

'Luckily, Sonia's English improved a lot quicker than Tim's Hebrew, but it looked as though she'd also underlined a few phrases for Tim's benefit. Take this from a conversation in the doctor's surgery: "Which contagious diseases have you had?" Or this one from the chapter entitled *In the camera shop*: "Please show me an enlarger".

'The experts tell us that 95 per cent of all communication is non-verbal. This is certainly the case whenever Tim had a hangover. But this theory seems to be confirmed today because I think you'd all agree with me that we don't need to be told that Tim and Sonia are very happy together – we only need to look at them.

'So perhaps I should stop talking altogether and let us communicate our love and best wishes to the happy couple in the most traditional and concrete of ways: with a toast. And here the Hebrew phrasebook comes in very handy – from page 20: "Leha'im!" – cheers!

'Ladies and gentlemen, please raise your glasses to the happy couple!'

Sample speech 15
Catchphrases

'Ladies and gentlemen, hello, good evening and welcome. Nice to see you, to see you nice!

'I am truly honoured to be here as Bruce's best man today – I'm not sure how high up his list of friends I'll be once this is over, but after so many years of friendship I guess he must have known what he was in for...

'Having known Bruce for so long – 20 years, man and boy – I have become almost immune to his cheesy one-liners. But as I was pondering them the other day I realized that now was my chance (you could say my Brucey bonus) to illustrate to him just how annoying all those clichés can be by incorporating as many as possible into my speech.

'So, for those of you who see Bruce and think, "seems like a nice boy", you may want to think again...

'I've never been able to get to the bottom of what it is about catchphrases that appeals to him so much – maybe it's an affliction that strikes all men blessed with the name Bruce. Perhaps we will never know.

'It all seemed to begin when we were at school. When asked once by the teacher, "Are you with us Bruce?", he replied: "No, I'm with the Woolwich," and as far as I can recall it was all downhill from there. Clearly he was watching too much TV from an early age (an obsession which shows no sign of abating).

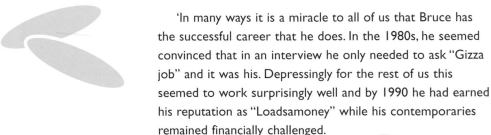

'In many ways it is a miracle to all of us that Bruce has the successful career that he does. In the 1980s, he seemed convinced that in an interview he only needed to ask "Gizza job" and it was his. Depressingly for the rest of us this seemed to work surprisingly well and by 1990 he had earned his reputation as "Loadsamoney" while his contemporaries remained financially challenged.

'One area of his life where his charms seemed to have less effect was his pursuit of the ladies. As Bruce was the one with the confidence and the charm (or so he thought), he would always be the one to make the first move. However, with lines ranging from the inanely annoying (such as, "Get your coat, you've pulled") to the downright offensive (see me later) it wasn't really surprising that we all had more than our fair share of drinks poured over us.

'In fact, the more I think about it the more I realize that my pitiful success with women was entirely down to Bruce. We'll be having a few words later mate...

'Still, you have to admire his perseverance, his robotic "I'll be back" attitude. Even when he was famously dumped for inappropriate use of "Cowabunga!" he remained unbowed, and the cheesy lines just kept on coming.

'So with such a penchant for dreadful chat up lines, how did he end up here today married to the beautiful Sally?

'"The truth is out there..." as Bruce himself might say. One thing I do know is that, from the moment he met her, he changed. Gone was the would-be womanizer ("You don't get anything for a pair, not in this game mate," I remember him telling me sadly as he burnt his little black book), to be replaced by what can only be described as a lovesick puppy ("Here's looking at you, kid").

'Sally, I don't think you need to worry about a mid life crisis for Bruce. For while most of us approach middle age with a growing sense of foreboding, for Bruce it just opens up a whole new repertoire of clichéd one-liners to try out on his family and friends.

'I shudder to think of the "mother-in-law" material he's got tucked up his sleeve, and only this morning he was heard to utter the immortal words "I don't believe it!" several times...

'Fortunately I can't imagine him getting away with phrases like "'Er indoors" too often, but I can't guarantee he won't try...

'Your wedding day is the happiest day of your life, a celebration of the start of a whole new chapter, an exciting but more grown-up stage of life. Let's not forget that we are here today to share in Bruce and Sally's joy at finding each other and to wish them every happiness for the future.

'My work is nearly done here, except to say "Hasta la vista baby!" Please raise your glasses and join me in a toast to: "the adorable couple"!'

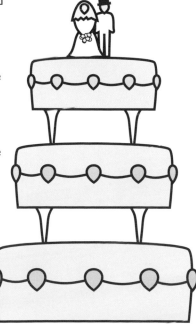

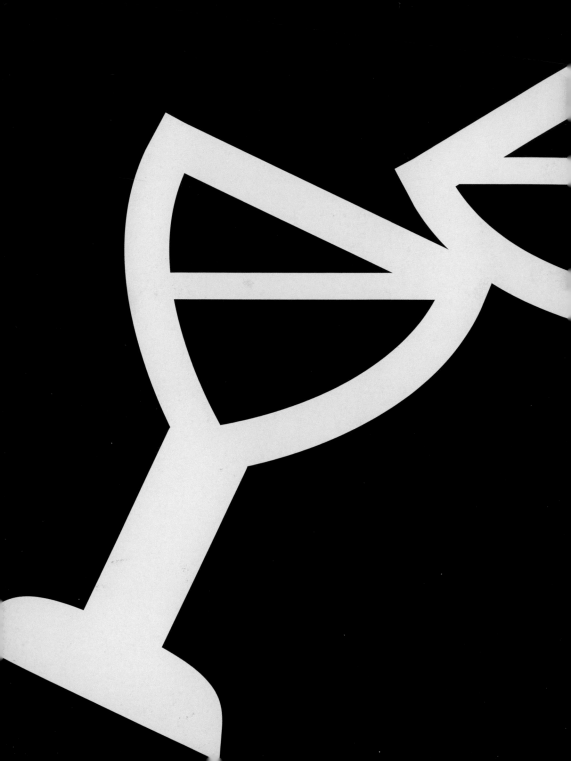

Sample

toasts

Traditional toasts

As best man it's your duty to end your speech with a toast to the bride and groom. To help you round off your speech with a flourish, choose a toast from this selection and adapt it to fit in smoothly with the rest of your material. Some couples don't want a series of long speeches at the reception and will ask you to make a simple toast instead. In fact, all wedding speeches are glorified toasts really, so if you're asked to give a toast only, think of it as a mini-speech. As best man, you may end up doing both if, for instance, there's a rehearsal dinner before the wedding, or post-wedding drinks for guests. Remember that the toast should come at the very end of your speech. You'll cause confusion if, after everyone has raised their glasses and made the toast, you then carry on speaking! Give everyone a moment to charge their glasses, be very clear in the exact wording of the toast: 'To the adorable couple!' Join in the toast... then sit down and enjoy the applause. Job done!

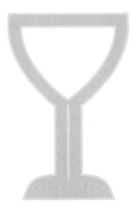

Who makes a toast?

There are no hard and fast rules today, of course, but the order of toasts/speeches traditionally runs as follows. Father of the bride, groom and best man.

The father of the bride The father of the bride usually makes the first speech or toast and ends by toasting the bride and groom.

The groom The groom toasts the bridesmaids/maid of honour. He may also choose to toast his wife and his in-laws.

The best man The best man replies to the groom's toast on behalf of the bridesmaids. He may also toast the bride's parents during his speech or 'absent friends' as he reads telegrams/messages from afar. His speech should end with a final toast to the happy couple.

Other toasts Increasingly, the bride, and sometimes also the chief bridesmaid will want to say a few words to mark the day. Generally, these toasts will come between those of the groom and best man.

Getting your toast right

Classic best man's toasts

'So I'd like you all to charge your glasses and join me in toasting the new **Mr and Mrs Brown**. Ladies and gentlemen, I give you the bride and groom.'

'Wishing them all the health, wealth and happiness in the world, I'd like you all to join me in toasting the happy couple. Ladies and gentlemen, the bride and groom.'

'Now it only remains for me to get you all on your feet. And with charged glasses [pause], I'd like you to join me in toasting the new **Mr and Mrs Roberts**. Ladies and gentlemen, I give you the wonderful bride and groom.'

'And now all I have left to do is to say what a privilege it is to ask you all to charge your glasses and – for those of you who still can! – rise to your feet. Ladies and gentlemen – the bride and groom.'

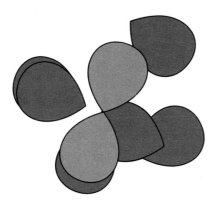

Do's and don'ts

- Do instruct the guests as to what to do. For example: 'Please raise your glasses with me...' Give them time to do so before you launch into the actual toast.
- Do tell guests exactly what the wording of the toast is to be, for example, 'To the bride and groom' or 'The happy couple!' etc.

Clarity is the key to a good toast.
- Do make your toast positive or funny.
- Do finish your toast with a flourish and leave them wanting more.
- Do, after the toast, sit when the guests sit down.
- Don't rush into a toast before your guests have had time to follow your

instructions or it will end up confused and only half-heard.
- Don't make your toast too long and complicated – or guests won't be able to follow it.

Amusing toasts

'Ladies and gentlemen, will you please join me now in toasting two young – well, quite young! – people who have everything, because (looking at couple) you love each other. Ladies and gentlemen, the lucky couple.'

'To finish with some words from the bard: "Love comforteth like sunshine after rain." So, you two, I hope your marriage is full of intermittent drizzle, followed by days of blistering heat. To the bride and groom.'

'Jerry – my best friend – here are some words of advice in the form of a wise old poem. "To keep a marriage brimming with love in the loving cup, when you are wrong, admit it, and when you are right, shut up!" To Jerry and Claire!'

'Here's to the two things that – without doubt – make a great marriage: a good sense of humour and selective hearing. Ladies and gentlemen – the bride and groom.'

'Before we toast the happy couple, here's to wives and lovers everywhere – and to them never, ever meeting!'

'If ever there was a competition for the best-suited couple, Posh and Becks needn't bother entering, because I think they're sitting at this table with me. No, not you Ted and Edith, I'm talking about the new Mr and Mrs Grimshaw. Ladies and gentlemen, it gives

me immense pleasure to ask you to raise your glasses
and toast – the bride and groom!'

'I'd like to end by toasting the bride and groom. But just
before I do, I want to quote some lines from a song to
the groom, Richard. The song was written many years
ago but the lyrics, I believe, are still meaningful today.
(Speak the words, with no tune). "She loves you, yeah,
yeah, yeah. She loves you, yeah, yeah, yeah, yeah. And
with a love like that, you know you should be glad."
'Ladies and gentlemen, I give you the bride and groom.'

'I asked my dad, joker that he is, what type of toast I
should propose at the wedding and he replied: "French".
Bon, sans vous faire attendre un instant de plus, Mesdames
et Messieurs, je vous présente... Monsieur et Madame
Jones. Les nouveaux mariés! A John et Jude!'

'In keeping with tradition, I'd like to say a few words
about the happy couple to end my speech. Everyone
who knows Paul knows that he likes having his own way
and I've always wondered what kind of woman he'd end
up with. Well, Alison is clever and beautiful and, when he
met her, Paul, in typical style, let her know who wears
the trousers early on. He looked her in the eye and said:
"You're the boss!" I knew then that she was the one for
him! So please join me in wishing Paul and Alison a
wonderful future together.'

More ideas for the toast

Beautifully brief

'It gives me tremendous pleasure to propose a toast to the bride and groom. My best friend has found the girl of his dreams and I really couldn't be happier for both of them. Please be upstanding for the bride and groom.'

True love

'Before I offer a toast to Tony and Marie, I'd like to leave you with one thought: You don't marry someone you can live with, you marry someone you can't live without. In this case, these two really have married the right person. To the bride and groom.'

'Just before I ask you to raise your glasses in a toast to the happy couple, I'd like to paraphrase an old adage. It goes: if you've got love in your lives, then that's great because you don't really need anything else. And if you haven't got love, it doesn't really matter what else you've got. To a couple always destined to have each other – Bob and Mary!'

A little bit more

'To end my speech I'd like to thank the parents of the bride and groom for giving us all such a good time. Everyone involved in this wedding has worked so hard to make it the great success that it is. I'd also like you to spare a thought for those friends and family who haven't been able to make it today. Many of them have sent their good wishes and I'm sure they're thinking of Julie and Duncan, not to mention the fabulous spread they're missing! But most of all, I'd like to propose we drink to Julie and Duncan. It's truly an honour to be best man at the wedding of such a fantastic couple. I hope you will join me in wishing them many, many years of happiness... To the bride and groom.'

Quick quip

'Ladies and gentlemen, please raise your glasses to the bride and groom. May all their joys be pure joys, and all their pain champagne.'

Index

About confetti.co.uk

Confetti.co.uk, founded in 1999, is the leading destination for brides- and grooms-to-be. Every month over 700,00 people visit www.confetti.co.uk to help them plan their weddings and special occasions. Here is a quick guide to our website

Weddings The wedding channel is packed full of advice and ideas to make your day more special and your planning less stressful. Our personalized planning tools will ensure you won't forget a thing.

Celebrations Checklists, advice and ideas for every party and celebration.

Fashion and beauty View hundreds of wedding, bridesmaid and party dresses and accessories. Get expert advice on how to look and feel good.

Travel Search for the most idyllic destinations for your honeymoon, wedding abroad or romantic breaks. Get fun ideas for hen and stag weekends.

Suppliers Thousands of suppliers to choose from including venues, gift lists companies, cake makers, florists and bridal retailers.

Café Talk to other brides and grooms and get ideas from our real life weddings section. Ask Aunt Betti, our agony aunt, for advice.

Shop All your wedding and party essentials in one place. The ranges include planning essentials, books and CDs, personalised stationery for weddings and celebrations, create your own trims, ribbons and papers, table decorations, party products including hen and stag, memories and gifts. If you'd like to do your shopping in person or view all the ranges before buying online, please visit the confetti stores.

Online

- Shop online 24 hours a day 7 days a week, use quick searches by department, product code or keyword, use the online order tracking facility and view brand new products as soon as they come out.
- Shop by phone on 0870 840 6060 Monday to Friday between 9 am and 5 pm.
- Shop by post by sending a completed order form to Confetti, Freepost NEA9292, Carr Lane, Low Moor, Bradford, BD12 0BR or fax on 01274 805 741.

By phone/freepost

Request your free copy of our catalogue online at www.confetti.co.uk or call 0870 840 6060

In store

London – 80 Tottenham Court Road, London, W1T 4TE

Leeds – The Light, The Headrow, Leeds, LS1 8TL

Birmingham – 43 Temple Street, Birmingham B2 5DP

Glasgow – 15–17 Queen Street, Glasgow, G1 3ED

Reading – 159 Friar Street, Reading, RG1 1HE

Executive Editor **Katy Denny**
Managing Editor **Clare Churly**
Executive Art Editor **Penny Stock**
Design **Cobalt id**
Production Manager **Ian Paton**